A RESEARCHER'S GUIDE TO BOSTON

"Washington St. from Winter St." view before 1872 fire
Courtesy of The Bostonian Society / Old State House

"Washington Street from Winter Street," view after 1872 fire
Boston, November 9 and 10, 1872
Courtesy of The Bostonian Society/Old State House

A RESEARCHER'S GUIDE TO BOSTON

Ann S. Lainhart

New England Historic Genealogical Society
www.NewEnglandAncestors.org
2003

International Standard Book Number: 0-88082-154-X
Library of Congress Control Number: 2003101423

Published by
New England Historic Genealogical Society
101 Newbury Street
Boston, MA 02116-3007
www.NewEnglandAncestors.org

Printed by McNaughton-Gunn, Inc., Saline, Michigan.

Reprinted July 2006.

CONTENTS

Introduction xi

Chapter 1 Getting Started 1

Chapter 2 Vital Records 3
Published 3
Unpublished 4
Obituaries 5
Divorces 6

Chapter 3 Church Records 7
Protestant 7
Catholic 10
Other Denominations and Guides 12

Chapter 4 Cemetery Records .15

Chapter 5 Town Records 19
Published 19
Unpublished 21
Records of the Poor 22

Chapter 6 Probate Records 31

Chapter 7 Land Records 35

Chapter 8 Court Records 37

Chapter 9 City Directories 41

Chapter 10 Military Records and Seaman's Records 43

Chapter 11 Tax Lists 49

Chapter 12 Business Papers, Account Books, and Diaries 51

Chapter 13 Censuses 55

Chapter 14 Voters' Lists 59

Chapter 15 Teachers' Records 63

Chapter 16 Passenger Lists 65

Chapter 17 Naturalizations 67

Chapter 18 Immigrants In Print .69

CONTENTS

Chapter 19 Some Miscellaneous Sources .73

Chapter 20 Boston In Print 75

Chapter 21 Towns That Are Now Part of Boston 81

Chapter 22 Articles on Boston Families .83

Chapter 23 Boston Area Repositories 91

Appendix One: Massachusetts Divorce Records,
Where to Find Them 95

Appendix Two: Ministers in Boston Up to 1846 99

Appendix Three: The Home for Destitute Catholic Children 109

Appendix Four: Boston Record Commissioners Report 113

Appendix Five: Inventory of the Estate of Amasa Davis 119

Appendix Six: 1860 Census Ward One, Boston 125

Appendix Seven: Examples From Institutional Records 131

Index 143

FIGURES

Page ii: "Washington Street from Winter Street" view before 1872 fire
Courtesy of The Bostonian Society / Old State House

Page iii: "Washington Street from Winter Street" view after 1872 fire, Boston, November 9 and 10, 1872
Courtesy of The Bostonian Society / Old State House

Page 11: "Methodist Church, Tremont Street," Boston, MA
Courtesy of the Bostonian Society / Old State House

Page 17: "Chatham St"
Courtesy of The Bostonian Society / Old State House

Page 25: "Bailey & Co. Views of Boston, The Blind Asylum, South Boston"
Courtesy of The Bostonian Society / Old State House

Page 33: "House of Amasa Davis"
NEHGS

Page 45: Image of Long Wharf
Courtesy of The Bostonian Society / Old State House

ABBREVIATIONS

ARCH   Massachusetts State Archives

BCA   Boston City Archives

BPL   Boston Public Library

FHL   Family History Libraries of the Church of Jesus Christ of Latter-day Saints

MHS   Massachusetts Historical Society

NARA   National Archives Records Administration – Northeast Region

NEHGS   New England Historic Genealogical Society

WPA   Works Progress Administration and Works Projects Administration

INTRODUCTION

My maternal grandmother died when I was thirteen years old. My grandfather sent all the family papers to my mother. I was fascinated that our ancestry traced back to the earliest years of settlements in New England, including Boston. These records sparked my interest and began my lifelong work in genealogy and history.

I volunteered at the New England Historic Genealogical Society (NEHGS) for a few weeks in the summer of 1977 and was offered a job there in December, just before I graduated from Sarah Lawrence College. I moved to Boston and began working as a reference librarian in January 1978 (just in time to experience the Blizzard of 1978!).

We lived in many different cities when I was growing up. My father worked for the Public Health Service (later NIOSH) and was subject to frequent transfer. I believe that one aspect of my love for genealogy is that it gave me roots and the feeling of being connected to certain places, even though I was constantly moving. My move to Boston felt like coming home. My fifth great-grandfather was Amasa Davis, who lived most of his life in Boston and was buried on the Boston Common. He was a merchant, and was Quartermaster General for Massachusetts. He had his portrait painted by Gilbert Stuart, and a piece of his Paul Revere tea set made it down to my grandparents. My great-great grandmother was Octavia Bryant from Florida. She was sent in the 1850s to her uncle's girls' school in Boston and her diaries tell about her life there. Her grandfather, James Bryant, was a cotton factor who lived on Bunker Hill in the early 1800s. The experience of tracing my own family began what would become a specialization in Boston research.

After researching in Boston for more than twenty-five years professionally, I hope I can help historians, genealogists, and researchers find and use these records pertaining to Boston and its inhabitants.

ACKNOWLEDGMENTS

I wish to thank Robert J. Dunkle, Jane Bramwell, Richard Andrew Pierce, Sandra Hewlett, Robert Charles Anderson, and Neil Todd for reading various drafts of this book. I wish to thank Alice Kane for information on the Boston Public Library; Melinde Lutz Sanborn for permission to reprint her article on the 1860 Ward 1 Boston census; Roger D. Joslyn for permission to reprint his article on divorces in Massachusetts; and Neil Todd for permission to print his list of Boston ministers. Thanks also go to Walter Hickey of the National Archives and Records Administration, Northeast Region; John F. McCauley of the Ancient and Honorable Artillery Company; Nancy Richard of The Bostonian Society; Karen L. Garvin of State Street Bank; and Marie E. Daly of NEHGS.

1 Getting Started

In most states, researchers begin at the state archives and/or the state historical society. That is also true in Massachusetts with the marvelous collections at the Massachusetts Archives (ARCH) and the Massachusetts Historical Society (MHS), but there is another very important repository. The New England Historic Genealogical Society (NEHGS) has one of the best collections of genealogies, local histories, and manuscripts for Massachusetts and New England. There is currently an informal agreement between NEHGS and MHS that whenever one of them receives a collection, it is evaluated for content. If the collection is deemed primarily genealogical, it belongs at NEHGS; if it is primarily historical, it belongs at MHS. Of course, the line between historical and genealogical sources is subjective, so any researcher must check both places for material of interest to their research.

Research on the city of Boston and its inhabitants should start at these three major repositories, but they by no means contain all the available sources for Boston research. Boston has been creating records for almost four hundred years, and few of these records have been centralized for preservation and ease of access. Records are located in many different city, state, and federal facilities, as well as private repositories. Access runs the gamut from unpublished and unindexed manuscripts to publications in book, microfilm, or electronic (CD) format. It is difficult to identify these sources, and even more difficult to locate them. The purpose of this book it to introduce the researcher to the many different sources, where to find them, and how to use them.

This book is arranged by record type. Beginning with the basic sources (vital, church, probate, land, and court records), this book continues through less-utilized records such as town, census, school, and voting lists, many of which have only recently become accessible to researchers. Other records,such as those of medical, correctional, and mental facilities have been accessible to researchers, but not well known.

For background on Boston through the centuries, there are several general sources (more references are in chapter twenty):

Robert Charles Anderson, "Focus on Boston," *Great Migration Newsletter*, 3:3.

Robert Charles Anderson, "Focus on Boston First Church," *Great Migration Newsletter*, 7:3.

Samuel Gardner Drake, *The History and Antiquities of Boston...from its Settlement in 1630, to the Year 1770* (Boston, 1856).

Darrett B. Rutman, *Winthrop's Boston, Portrait of A Puritan Town, 1630–1649* (Williamsburg,VA, 1865).

Justin Winsor, *The Memorial History of Boston, Including Suffolk County, Massachusetts, 1630–1880*, 4 volumes (Boston, 1880–1881).

Harold Kirker, *Bulfinch's Boston, 1787–1817* (New York, 1964).

Michael Price and Anthony Mitchell Sammarco, *Boston's Immigrants 1840–1925* (Charleston, SC, 2000).

Thomas H. O'Connor, *Fitzpatrick's Boston, 1846–1866: John Bernard Fitzpatrick, Third Bishop of Boston* (Boston, 1984).

Chapter twenty-two lists many articles on Boston families; by studying these articles, even though they may not be the family of particular interest to you, may give you clues for how to approach your own research.

2 VITAL RECORDS

PUBLISHED

The seventeenth-century vital records of Boston were published in 1883 as volume nine of the Record Commissioners Reports. This volume contains the birth, marriage, and death records from the town clerk's records and the baptismal records of the First Church. The introduction says:

> For most of the years before 1700 the record of the births seems to be quite full and complete; but sometimes, as in 1675, nearly all was lost by some chance. The years 1647–50 are also evidently imperfect. The deaths and marriages are less regularly recorded, and there is a long break in each. No deaths were recorded 1665–88, and no marriages 1663–79.

The eighteenth-century births and marriages were published in three volumes of the Record Commissioners Reports. Volume twenty-one, published in 1894, contains the births from 1700 to 1800; Volume twenty-eight, published in 1898, contains the marriages from 1700 to 1751; and Volume thirty, published in 1903, contains the marriages from 1752 to 1809. These three volumes contain only the births and marriages from the town clerk's records.

The town clerk in the eighteenth century did not keep records of deaths, but information on deaths for Boston residents can be found in a variety of sources such as old sexton's bills, death notices, obituaries, estate notices from newspapers, church records, diaries, vital records of other towns, and cemeteries, some of which have been published separately. *Deaths in Boston 1700 to 1799* (Dunkle and Lainhart, 1999) has combined deaths found in many of these varied sources.

In the July 1997 (151:343) issue of *The New England Historical and Genealogical Register* (NEHGR) David F. March published "Deaths in Boston: Decedents Reported in the *Boston Medical and Surgical Journal*, 1828–1829." He has arranged the deaths alphabetically and almost all of them give the age at death. Helen Schatvet Ullmann published in the *Register* "A Few Deaths in Boston, 1760–1772" (155:419).

UNPUBLISHED

In the records of the Superior Court of Judicature (ARCH) there is a small volume labeled "Court Files Suffolk Births, Marriages, and Deaths Jan 1637/8 to Aug 1774." Much of this volume consists of returns by ministers of the marriages they have performed, but the volume also contains depositions like this one dated 14 November 1728:

> Simon Willard of full Age Testify's what he Remember of Children & Grand Children of John Ingersoll deceased Reputed Son of Richard Ingersoll of Salem Deceased (as I have heard) 1 Johns Children Samuel Mary & Ruth 2d Nathal. Children were John Widow Kinghts 3d Richard his Children were Richard who Dyed & left three Children Two Sons and a Daughter who is married to Daniel Creasy 4th Samuel his Children one was Wife to Thomas Beadle the now Wife of Josiah Orn 5th Ruth her Child was Ruth 6th Aged William Ropes his wife yet Living

At the end of the eighteenth century very few births were being recorded with the town clerk, and this trend continued into the mid-nineteenth century. In the early eighteenth century the town clerk did not keep death records, so from 1800 to 1848 the most comprehensive vital records recorded were marriages. The records from 1801 to 1848 are available at the City of Boston Registry Archives and on microfilm or microfiche at FHL and NEHGS. The Boston Registry Archives also has city records of births, marriages, and deaths past 1848. [The city of Boston has two archives; one is in the City Hall and is called the City of Boston Registry Archives; the other is in the Hyde Park section of Boston and is called Boston City Archives.]

In 1841, Massachusetts passed a law requiring towns to keep records of all births, marriages, and deaths, and to send copies of the records to a central office in Boston. Boston did not comply until 1848, so for records from 1841 to 1848, one must search the city records. From 1848 to 1910, manuscript copies and microfilm copies of all Boston vital records sent to the central office will be found at the ARCH and microfilm copies will be found at NEHGS, BPL, and FHL. The current law allows for another five years of vital records to be moved to the ARCH every five years.

The late nineteenth- and early twentieth-century copies of city death records give the name of the undertaker and the cemetery where the deceased is buried, while the state copy does not. The state copy may contain miscopied information, so if there is any question, it is best to check the city record.

Vital records from 1916 to the present will be found at the Registry of Births, Marriages, and Deaths in Boston City Hall, or at the state Registry of Vital Records and Statistics in Dorchester. Some of these records are restricted and cannot be viewed. These restricted records include births where no father is listed, the birth records of stillborn children, original birth certificates for children later adopted, originals of records later amended, births of undetermined sex, and marriage records of underage children when the parents have requested that the record be sealed (these restrictions do not apply to the records transferred to ARCH). The state office has certain hours each day when researchers may use the records for a small hourly fee. Researchers may copy information from the certificates for no charge beyond the researching fee, or they may purchase certified copies (the only type of copies provided by this office).

OBITUARIES

The following volumes cover all extant Boston newspapers for the time period. There are several published lists or indexes to the obituaries and death notices from Boston newspapers.

Index of Obituaries in Boston Newspapers, 1704–1800

Volume 1, *Deaths Within Boston, A-Z*

Volume 2, *Deaths Outside Boston, A-Johnson, Chloe*

Volume 3, *Deaths Outside Boston, Johnson, Daniel-Z*

The death notices and obituaries for those outside of Boston generally are for well known people or those who died an unusual death as the following examples show:

Loring, Nicholas, Rev. at North Yarmouth, left wid. & 10 ch., 31 July 1763.

McClure, Thomas, of Brookfield, murdered by Jabez Green during a quarrel, 6 Oct 1741.

Owens, Morgan, killed by Indians near Walkie, Orange Co., NJ,[sic] 28 Feb 1756.

Reed, William, born in Londonderry, Ireland, executed for piracy at Newport, RI, 19 July 1723, ae 35y.

Robbins, Wife of Wait, of Weathersfield, CT, killed in a tornado with her 10 year old boy, 25 Aug 1787.

Strong, Supply, at Litchfield, CT, ae 90y, was the 2d male child born in Lebanon, 1 Nov 1792.

Vining, John, Hon., in Salem Co., PA, [sic; prob. Salem NJ], speaker of the House of Assembly, 13 Nov 1770.

Index of Marriages and Deaths in Massachusetts Centinel, 1784–1790, and Columbian Centinel, 1790–1840.

This was a WPA(Works Progress Administration) project and covers the period from March 24, 1784, to April 29, 1840. The marriage volumes include nearly 80,000 marriages; 27% for marriages in Boston, 40% for marriages in Massachusetts except Boston, 16% for marriages in New England except Massachusetts, and 17% for marriages in the rest of the country.

Index to Obituary Notices in the Boston Transcript, 1875–1899, 2 vols.

This set also includes the Boston Advertiser for 1875–1884. This index was begun in 1926 with volunteers and then continued under the WPA. It lists just the name of the deceased, death date, and the newspaper issue date. Generally the information in these volumes was in the newspaper death notice, but sometimes there is more information in the actual newspaper.

Index to Obituary Notices in the Boston Transcript, 1900–1930, 3 vols.

This set contains the name of the deceased, the death date, and the newspaper issue date. Many of these listings are simple death notices and others are long obituaries.

DIVORCES

The records of the Superior Court of Judicature at ARCH contain a volume of divorces from 1760 to 1786. Though the language has changed, the reasons for divorces certainly have not changed in the past 400 years, as this case from 10 December 1772 shows:

> James Richardson of Leominster...Husband of Hannah Richardson...that on [10 January 1753] he was lawfully married...to the said Hannah...that on the fifth day of May last the said Hannah...had lacivious, lewd, wanton, wicked and unlawful intercourse and familiarty with one Abel Joy...that the said Hannah ever since her intermarriage with this proponent hath lived in a continual course of criminal intercourse with lewd and wicked men and hath maliciously threatned and sought to destroy this proponents fortune and Estate, burn his House, Maim his Children and attempted to take away his life.

Roger D. Joslyn wrote an article on divorces in Massachusetts which first appeared in the *Newsletter of the Massachusetts Genealogical Council*, and is reprinted with permission of the author, in Appendix One.

3 CHURCH RECORDS

PROTESTANT

The seventeenth-century records for the First Church in Boston are included with the vital records in Volume 9 of the Record Commissioners Report. For an interesting study of the First Church of Boston in the seventeenth century, see Melinde Lutz Sanborn, "Reverend James Allen's Church Census of 1688," in *Great Migration Newsletter*, Volume 7, No. 1.

Church records became very important in the later eighteenth century and early nineteenth century because fewer births were recorded by the Boston town clerk. Therefore, you are more likely to find a baptismal record than a birth record in this time period.

The following Boston churches have published records. The years listed indicate the years for which records are included in the published material. Many of these churches continued after the end date listed below; some are still in existence. These records are also included in Robert J. Dunkle and Ann S. Lainhart "The Records of the Churches of Boston," a NEHGS CD.

Richard D. Pierce, *Records of the First Church of Boston*, in Publications of The Colonial Society of Massachusetts, (1961) Vols. 39–41.

Andrew Oliver & James Bishop Peabody, *Records of Trinity Church, Boston, 1728–1830*, in Publications of The Colonial Society of Massachusetts, (1980) Vols. 55–56.

Thomas Bellows Wyman, edited by Robert J. Dunkle and Ann S. Lainhart, *The New North Church, Boston, 1714–1799*, (Baltimore, 1995).

Robert J. Dunkle and Ann S. Lainhart, *Hollis Street Church, Boston; Records of Admissions, Baptisms, Marriages and Deaths, 1732–1887*, (Boston, 1998).

New Brick Church, NEHGR, Vols. 18–19.

West Church, NEHGR, Vols. 91-94

The CD from NEHGS also includes the records of the other Boston churches that were founded before 1800: Second or Old North Church (1676–1816), First Baptist (1665–1879), Old South (1669–1875), King's Chapel (1703–1844), Brattle Street (1699–1804), New South (1719–1812), New Brick (1722–1776), Christ Church (1723–1851), Federal Street (now Arlington Street) (1730–1865), Second Baptist (1743–1811), New North (1714–1816), and Baldwin Place (1769–1881) as well as the First Church, Second Parish, and Third Parish of Roxbury.

For the following churches founded after 1800, there are transcripts in the Boston City Hall Archives and on microfilm at NEHGS and FHL. Most of these transcripts are indexed by surname only:

Pine Street Church (1834–1865)

First Universalist Church (1813–1840)

First Christian Church (1803–1870)

Bromfield Street Church (1838–1854)

Charles Street Baptist Church (1807–1865)

Park Street Church (1810–1877)

Second Universalist Church (1815–1856)

New Jerusalem Church (1827–1879)

St. Paul's Church (1820–1860)

Twelfth Congregational Church (1825–1862)

Purchase Street Church (1826–1859)

Pitts Street Chapel (1835–1845)

Grace Church (1828–1865)

Phillips Church, South Boston (1825–1887)

Hawes Place Church, South Boston (1823–1878)

St. Matthew's Church, South Boston (1817–1837)

Also, there are transcripts of these churches in towns that became part of Boston:

First Church, Charlestown (1632–1789 — not indexed)

Second Congregational Church, Charlestown (1817–1827 — not indexed)

Harvard Church, Charlestown (1840–1889)

Church Records

First Church, Dorchester (1729–1845)

First Church, West Roxbury (1712–1837)

First Baptist Church, Roxbury (1821–1884)

Many of these transcripts also include admission and dismission records that are very important but often overlooked by researchers. These records can indicate when people moved from one Boston church to another, or where people came from when they suddenly appeared in Boston, or where they went when they disappeared from Boston. In the records of the New North Church from 1714 to 1799, there are many admissions and dismissions to and from other Boston churches. There are also admissions and dismissions to and from churches in forty-eight other towns, most of which were in Massachusetts. Represented in these records are the counties of Essex, Middlesex, Worcester, Bristol, and Barnstable. Towns in Connecticut, Maine, and New Hampshire, as well as Huntington, Long Island, and Marietta, Ohio, are also represented. There is also the case of William Downs who was received by dismission from a church in London. Some of these records have comments like "was removed having joined the Baptists," "had gone over to the Church of England," and "formerly of the English Church."

Boston civil marriage records usually name the justice of the peace or the minister who performed the ceremony. But in the case of ministers, the records do not usually list the name of the church where the marriage occured. By identifying the church, you may then be led to baptismal records, admissions, and dismissions. To determine with which church a minister was affiliated in the colonial period, consult Frederick Lewis Weis's *Colonial Clergy of New England* (1936). For ministers through the mid-nineteenth century, consult John Hayward's 1849 *A Gazetteer of Massachusetts*, which has a section called "Boston Churches and Ministers," or "A Complete List of the Ministers of Boston of all Denominations, From 1630 to 1842" in Volume 1 of *The New England Historical and Genealogical Register*. The list in the *Gazetteer* is organized by church, and the *Register* lists the ministers chronologically. Drawing from the *Gazetteer*, Neil Todd has prepared an alphabetical list of the ministers and the churches with which they were affiliated (see Appendix Two).

For ministers after the mid-nineteenth century, check the city directory for the year of the marriage either under the name of the minister (which may list the church with which he is affiliated) or in the section that lists the churches (which may also list their ministers).

In 1889, Carroll D. Wright published *Report on the Custody and Condition of the Public Records of Parishes, Towns, and Counties*, which surveyed the records of both existing and extinct churches in Massachusetts. This report may help you determine what records were then available for a particular Boston church, and whether records exist for an extinct church. If the people you are researching belonged to a Congregational church, then consult Harold Field Worthley's *An Inventory of the Records of the Particular (Congregational) Churches of Massachusetts* (rev. ed. 1975). He covers the following Boston churches:

First Church

Second Church (The Old North Church)

Third Church (Old South Church)

French Huguenot Church, extinct

King's Chapel

Fourth Church (Brattle Street or Brattle Square or The Manifesto Church), extinct

Fifth Church (New North Church), extinct

Sixth Church (New South Church), extinct

Seventh Church (New Brick Church), extinct

Arlington Street Church (originally Presbyterian)

Eighth Church (Hollis Street Church), extinct

Ninth Church (The West or Lynde Street Church), extinct

Tenth Church (Samuel Mather's Church), extinct

Eleventh Church (School Street or Rev. Andrew Croswell's Church) extinct

When you are interested in the records of an existing church, always call or write the church before going there, as the church offices may not be open every day. Also, the church may not store all their records on site; they may be on deposit in an archive or library or even a bank vault. To use the records on deposit, you may need written permission from the church. The church may also have a particular member who deals with questions of history or early records. Therefore, it is best to contact the church by phone or mail to find out about their records for a particular time period and to make an appointment, if necessary, to use the records.

CATHOLIC

At the Archives of the Archdiocese of Boston are the records of most of the Boston area Catholic parishes. Be sure to consult James M. O'Toole's *Guide to the Archives of the Archdiocese of Boston*. The Archives of the Archdiocese requests that people call ahead for an appointment, so they can have the material ready to be searched. These are primarily pre-1900 records; for later

"Methodist Church, Tremont Street, Boston, MA"
Courtesy of the Bostonian Society / Old State House

records, the individual parishes must be contacted directly. The following is a
list of the parish records at the Archives and the year the records begin:

Cathedral of the Holy Cross, 1788

St. Mary, Charlestown, 1828

St. Mary, North End, 1834

St. Patrick, South End, 1836

St. Stephen (St. John the Baptist), North End, 1843

St. Peter and Paul, South Boston, 1844

Holy Trinity (German), South End, 1844

Most Holy Redeemer (St. Nicholas), East Boston, 1844

St. Joseph, Roxbury, 1845

These records are for baptisms and marriages; parishes seldom recorded
deaths or burials. Although the volumes are rarely indexed, surnames in the
margins make them easy to search. This common feature of most volumes
allows the researcher to quickly search unindexed records by glancing down
the margins for a particular surname.

Catholic records possess the helpful feature of recording sponsors at baptisms
and witnesses at marriages, and these people are frequently relatives.
Checking the sponsors or witnesses at other people's baptisms and marriages
is often a good way to find relatives.

The Archives of the Archdiocese has the records and a typescript history of
the Home for Destitute Catholic Children, and is happy to answer any questions about the records. The Archives will provide specific information on
individuals where names and reasonably accurate dates are known, but it cannot conduct extensive research. The children at the Home were rarely
orphans; typically, one parent was alive but in a situation that did not allow
them to take care of children, such as being ill, in jail, or intemperate. For
more information, see my article in Appendix Three. The Archives also has
the records of nineteenth-century Catholic orphanages in Boston, and more
information on these can be found in *Guide to the Archives of the Archdiocese
of Boston* by James M. O'Toole.

OTHER DENOMINATIONS AND GUIDES

In the Boston area there are six church archives or libraries which may have
the early records of an existing church or the records of an extinct church.
They are:

The Congregational Library, 14 Beacon Street, Boston, MA 02108

The Diocesan Library and Archives, The Episcopal Diocese of Massachusetts, 138 Tremont St., Boston, MA 02111

(Catholic) Archives of the Archdiocese of Boston, 2121 Commonwealth Ave., Brighton, MA 02135

(Methodist) Boston University School of Theology Library, 745 Commonwealth Ave., Boston, MA 02215

(Unitarian-Universalist) Harvard Divinity School Library, 45 Francis Ave., Cambridge, MA 02138

American Jewish Historical Society Library, 160 Herrick Road, Newton Centre, MA 02459

The records for New England Quaker meetings are at the Rhode Island Historical Society in Providence, Rhode Island.

The following guides and histories are published for the different denominations:

Baptist

Brush, John Woolman, *Baptists in Massachusetts* (Valley Forge, 1970).

Eaton, Rev. W.H., *Historical Sketch of the Massachusetts Baptist Missionary Society and Convention, 1802–1902* (Boston: Massachusetts Baptist Convention, c. 1903).

McLaughlin, W.G., *New England Dissent, 1630–1833, The Baptists and Separation of Church and State* (Cambridge, 1971).

Catholic

O'Toole, J.M., *Guide to the Archives of the Archdiocese of Boston* (New York, 1982).

Congregational

Clark, Joseph S., *A Historical Sketch of the Congregational Churches in Massachusetts from 1620 to 1858* (Boston, 1858).

Morgan, Mary Frederica Rhinelander, *Manuscript Collections of The Congregational Library at Boston: A Survey* (1982).

Taylor, Richard H., *The Churches of Christ of the Congregational Way in New England* (Benton Harbor, Michigan, 1989).

Episcopal

Duffy, Mark J., *Guide to the Parochial Archives of the Episcopal Church in Boston* (Boston, 1981).

Tyng, D., *Massachusetts Episcopalians, 1607–1957* (Boston, 1960).

Jewish

Ehrenfried, Albert, *A Chronicle of Boston Jewry from the Colonial Settlement to 1900* (Boston, 1963).

Sarna, Jonathan and Ellen Smith, *The Jews of Boston* (1995).

Schindler, Solomon, *Israelites in Boston: A Tale Describing the Development of Judaism in Boston* (Boston, 1889).

Quaker

Selleck, George A., *Quakers in Boston* (Cambridge, 1976).

Unitarian-Universalist

Miller, Russell E., *The Larger Hope: The First Century of the Universalist Church in America, 1770–1870* (Boston, 1979).

4 CEMETERY RECORDS

A *Guide to Massachusetts Cemeteries* by David Allen Lambert (NEHGS, 2002) has one hundred and eleven entries for Boston, though some listings are for different sections of a large cemetery. This book notes if the inscriptions have been published or are in manuscript form. It also includes the phone numbers if there is a cemetery office.

The four major cemeteries, Copp's Hill, Granary, Central, and King's Chapel, have published inscriptions:

> Bridgman, Thomas, *The Pilgrims of Boston and Their Descendants*: With an Introduction by Hon. Edward Everett. LL.D., Also, *Inscriptions from the Monuments in the Granary Burial Ground, Tremont Street* (New York, 1856).

> *Gravestone Inscriptions and Records of the Tomb Burials in the Granary Burying Ground*, Boston, Mass. (Salem, 1918).

> *Gravestone Inscriptions and Records of the Tomb Burials in the Central Burying Ground, Boston Common, and Inscriptions in The South Burying Ground*, Boston (Salem, 1817).

> Bridgman, Thomas, *Memorials of The Dead in Boston; Containing Exact Transcripts of Inscriptions on the Sepulchral Monuments in the King's Chapel Burial Ground, In the City of Boston* (Boston, 1853).

> Whitmore, William H., *The Graveyards of Boston, First Volume, Copp's Hill Epitaphs* (Albany, 1878).

Inscriptions and Records of The Old Cemeteries in Boston (Dunkle and Lainhart, NEHGS, 2000) combines the inscriptions of these four cemeteries in one volume, with Hawes Street and South or Boston Neck cemeteries and with new material from manuscripts at the Boston Parks Department and Boston Public Library.

For resources on recent cemeteries (which can be quite large, such as Mt. Auburn or Forest Hills), you need to contact the cemetery office, which is often open only on weekdays, to get a map to find the grave or plot of interest to you. Be sure to check whatever records are in the office, because they may have more information than the actual gravestones. Several years ago, I went to photgraph the gravestones in a plot at Mt. Auburn Cemetery for a client. The cards in the office listed about twelve people buried in this plot with names, ages, and burial dates, but the plot itself was a big boulder with a plaque affixed to it bearing just the family surname. A lot of help that was to the client!

There are two collections that contain photographs of New England gravestones. In the manuscript collection at NEHGS is Harriette M. Forbes' "New England Gravestones, 1653–1800." At the American Antiquarian Society in Worcester is the Farber Gravestone Collection of Daniel Farber, Jessie Lye Farber, and Harriette M. Forbes. This collection was recently published on eleven CDs.

Richard Andrew Pierce recently published *The Stones Speak: Irish Place Names from Inscriptions in Boston's Mount Calvary Cemetery* (Boston, 2000). Gravestones for those born in Ireland may sometimes give the county or place of birth.

Catholics in Boston up to 1860 were buried mainly in five cemeteries. The first, St. Augustine Cemetery in South Boston, opened in 1819 (though burials may have started as early as 1805); second was the Bunker Hill or Charlestown Catholic Cemetery in 1834; third was Cambridge Catholic Cemetery in 1845; fourth was St. Joseph Cemetery in Roxbury in 1852; and finally Mt. Auburn or Sand Banks Catholic Cemetery in 1854. You may find members of the same family buried in more than one of these cemeteries.

Marie E. Daly is preparing a database of the Charlestown Catholic Cemetery that will eventually be on the NEHGS website. This cemetery contains many pauper burials. For the other burials there are one hundred and fifty-one tombstones and records of the lot sales. To the information from the cemetery, Daly added whatever information she could find in vital records, naturalization records, passenger lists, and city directories. The database now has about two thousand people associated with this cemetery. The lot sales were from 1830 to 1845, with the burials from 1834 to the 1890s; therefore most of these people were pre-famine Irish.

As mentioned above, the city copies of death records provide the names of the undertaker and cemetery. Patrick Denver was the undertak er for many of these burials in Charlestown, but he was also the undertaker for many of the burials in Cambridge Catholic Cemetery. Daly has found that on the death records, Denver sometimes mixed up the cemetery in which the burial took place. So if you cannot find someone buried in Charlestown, try Cambridge.

On July 25, 1844, the Jewish Congregation Ohabei Shalom purchased land in East Boston for the first Jewish cemetery in greater Boston. Previously, the closest Jewish cemeteries were in Newport, Rhode Island, and Albany, New York. The Jewish Cemetery Association of Massachusetts has established a database for all Jewish burials in the greater Boston area. The database currently contains over sixty-five thousand individual entries from sixty-two cemeteries. For more information, consult Warren Blatt's *Resources for Jewish Genealogy in the Boston Area.*

"Chatham St"
Courtesy of The Bostonian Society / Old State House

5 TOWN RECORDS

PUBLISHED

We are very fortunate that the Boston Record Commissioners Reports contains both the records of the Boston Selectmen's meetings and town meetings through 1822. They have also published a variety of records relating to Boston from the seventeenth- to the early-nineteenth century. The following list shows what each volume contains and explains the contents of the additional records. Volumes not included in this list either contain vital records or records of towns which later became part of Boston; these volumes are discussed in other chapters.

Volume 1, [Seventeenth-century tax lists] (1881)

Volume 2, *Boston Records, 1634–1660, and the Book of Possessions* (1881)

Volume 5, [miscellaneous records] (1884)
"In their fourth report...the Record Commissioners announced that the City Council had appropriated the sum of five thousand dollars for the publication of historical documents relating to Boston...the first of the volumes thus ordered is the present fifth report, and it contains a series of articles relating to the history of estates lying on or around Beacon Hill. These articles were contributed in 1855 to the 'Boston Daily Transcript,' by the late Nathaniel Ingersoll Bowditch, under the signature of 'Gleaner.'" These "Gleaner" articles describe how original grants of land have been divided up into the lots found in 1855.

Volume 7, *Boston Records from 1660 to 1701* (1881)

Volume 8, *Boston Records from 1700 to 1728* (1883)

Volume 10, *Miscellaneous Papers* (1886)
This volume contains several small documents from the seventeenth and very early eighteenth centuries. One of the documents is a "census" of Boston in 1707; it lists the name of the head of household, the number of polls in the

household, the number of negroes in the household, and if the person is a renter, the amount of the rent and the name of the owner of the property. There are some interesting details included: Eliza Chaffin, widow, and Jno McKenzy are listed as renters on property "Estate of old mrs adams Just Dead & so not setled"; Jno Needham was renting a house and shop from "young Josiah Munjey at Charlstown"; and Rd Stratton "ye Miller" was renting from "broughtons Daughters."

Another document is "Admissions to the Town of Boston, 1670–1700" and includes entries like July 31, 1682: "Phillip Gosse came from Roxbury with a vitious ffamilie, of wch Mary Wood is or was one of his seruants who hath had a Bastard & are entertained by Joseph Holmes"; October 30, 1682 "An Tilige, a woman yt hath a husband at Nevis lodgeth at Jns Brookens and refuseth to goe to her husband"; and April 27, 1680 "Thomas Bittle, Cartr at Jera sergeant, Sd to be very prophane & of a bad report."

Volume 11, *Records of Boston Selectmen, 1701 to 1715* (1884)

Volume 12, *Boston Records from 1729 to 1742* (1885)

Volume 13, *Records of Boston Selectmen, 1716 to 1736* (1885)

Volume 14, *Boston Town Records, 1742 to 1757* (1885)

Volume 15, *Boston Town Records, 1736 to 1742* (1886)

Volume 16, *Boston Town Records, 1758 to 1769* (1886)

Volume 17, *Selectmen's Minutes from 1742–3 to 1753* (1887)

Volume 18, *Boston Town Records, 1770 through 1777* (1887)

Volume 19, *Selectmen's Minutes from 1754 through 1763* (1887)

Volume 20, *Selectmen's Minutes from 1764 through 1768* (1889)

Volume 22, *The Statistics of the United States Direct Tax of 1798, as Assessed on Boston; and The Names of the Inhabitants of Boston in 1790, as Collected for the First National Census.* (1890)

The 1798 direct tax is a good substitute for the missing 1800 Federal census. This tax includes information on land owners and descriptions of the land and buildings.

Volume 23, *Selectmen's Minutes from 1769 through April, 1775* (1893)

Volume 25, *Selectmen's Minutes from 1776 through 1786* (1894)

Volume 26, *Boston Town Records, 1778 to 1783* (1895)

Volume 27, *Selectmen's Minutes from 1789 through 1798* (1896)

Volume 29, *Miscellaneous Papers* (1900)

Contains several documents including papers relating to the Great Fire of 1700, which lists both the real and personal estate lost by particular persons.

For example, Elisabeth Allcock lost "One large warehouse at Olivers dock newly repair's with a new Shed adjoining"; John Allen, cordwainer, lost a house which included three tenements and lists the inventory of his house and all he owned; "and Rebecca Amory lost in the late Fire a house & Shop in Mackrel Lane, the House occupied by Mr Stamp rented for Eight pound p ann. & the Shop occupied by Mr Graham rented for Two Pounds thirteen shillings & 4d a year."

This volume also includes "Port Arrivals and Immigrants to the City of Boston, 1715–1716 and 1762–1769" which was reprinted as a separate volume in 1973 by Genealogical Publishing Company.

Volume 31, *Boston Town Records, 1784 to 1796* (1903)

Volume 32, *A Volume Relating to the Early History of Boston Containing the Aspinwall Notarial Records from 1644 to 1651* (1903)

Volume 33, *Minutes of the Selectmen's Meetings 1799 to, and including, 1810* (1904)

Volume 35, *Boston Town Records, 1796 to 1813* (1905)

Volume 37, *Boston Town Records, 1814 to 1822* (1906)

Volume 38, *Minutes of the Selectmen's Meetings, 1811 to 1817, and Part of 1818* (1908)

3 39, *Minutes of the Selectmen's Meetings from September 1, 1818, to April 24, 1822* (1909)

Brigitte Burkett has published *Genealogical Data Extracted from the Boston Selectmen's Minutes*, 1736–1775 (Heritage Books, 1993).

For more information on the Boston Record Commissioners Reports and examples of what can be found on just one family, see Appendix Four for an article I wrote for *The Essex Genealogist*, August 1999 (19:131-4), reprinted with their permission.

UNPUBLISHED

Boston was incorporated as a city in 1822 and changed from having selectmen to a city council. The records of council meetings are at the BCA.

Carroll D. Wright's 1889 publication *Report on the Custody and Condition of the Public Records of Parishes, Towns, and Counties* lists town records then in the custody of the town clerk. The list includes town proceedings 1674–1822, Board of Aldermen 1822–1885, Common Council 1822–1885, Assessors 1780–1885 (those before 1780 were destroyed by fire), Selectmen 1701–1822, and Proprietors 1634–1728. Many records were published in the Record Commissioners Report (see above). Unpublished records may be found at the BCA or the Boston City Hall Archives. Wright also lists the records of towns annexed by Boston: Brighton, Charlestown, Dorchester, Roxbury, and West Roxbury. Again, the unpublished records of these towns are probably at the BCA or the Boston City Hall Archives.

RECORDS OF THE POOR

In the seventeenth, eighteenth, and nineteenth centuries, each town in Massachusetts was responsible for the care of recognized inhabitants who fell on hard times. A large port city like Boston would also have many transients in need of help and care. In the town records is a 1768 directive to take Richard Swansbury to the almshouse because he was "not an Inhabitant of any Town in this Province nor having the wherewithall to support himself." And in 1680, Benjamin Gillam bound himself to the Town Treasurer to ensure that William Wharton "Shall not be Chargeable to the Sd towne," which indicates that William Wharton was not from Boston.

In Volume 10 of the Record Commissioners Reports table of contents is a document labeled "Admissions to the Town of Boston, 1670–1700" This title is misleading, since the term "admitted" implies that these people became inhabitants of Boston. In fact, this volume contains "A List of Seuerall psons returned to ye Countie Courts at seuerall times not admitted nor aproued of by ye select men of Boston to be Inhabitants of ye Towne" and a series of bonds given by recognized inhabitants to make sure that "certain intending settlers shall not become chargeable to the town." In these two parts, the "intending settlers" are listed by name, and sometimes occupation or from whence they came. Many are from other Massachusetts towns or New England colonies, but there are also arrivals from "Newyorke," "Barbado," "Jamaca," "Nevis," Virginia, "New found Land," England, Scotland, Portugal, Long Island, and "Caralina." In some cases there is additional information:

John Brice & Wm. Lane both came affoote from Mary Land to Milford whethr Runawayes or Roman Catholiks uknownd, at John Wings.

An Perry, formerly Sheffield, hauinge left ye Towne a considerable time & an Inhabitant in another place beinge reported of euill life & behauiour was returned to ye Court.

Jacob Sayer a young man came from New Yorke at Edward Cowells reported to be run fr. his Master in Virginia.

John Lee an Inhabitant of Ipswich, after warned out of ye towne yet remaines, removinge from place to place.

Eliza fford saith she hath a Husband at Newyorke lately d/d. here of a Child and accordinge to a certificate herewith a very bad woman, came hither from Road Island.

Martha Smallage came from Longe Island who in abscence of her husband Smalledge, went to Long Island, was thre maryed to another man, hath liued with him a considerable time is now big wth Child by him & latelie brought hither by her first husband who is since gone to sea; lodgeth at ye widdow Blowes.

Feb. 2, 1681–82. Robert Walker, weaver, became surety to the town for Edward Crookes, weaver, and his family. ["Robert Walker came to the selectmen's meeting, Feb. 25, 1683, and affirmed that Edw. Crooks hath been gon out of this towne nine months and is informed he is accepted at Stoneingtown as an Inhabitant." - Side note in original.]

In the *Publications of The Colonial Society of Massachusetts*, Lawrence W. Towner published "The Indentures of Boston's Poor Apprentices: 1734–1805" (43[1966]:417-67). The selectmen had authority to apprentice out the children of the town's poor to learn a trade (for the boys) or housewifery or spinning (for the girls). The boys' trades ran the gamut of colonial industry: shoemaker, tailor, blacksmith, victualler, shipwright, farmer, barber, ropemaker, bricklayer, perucke maker, navigator, weaver, housewright, goldsmith, cabinet maker, baker, chair maker, cooper, surveyor, and tobacconist. As Mr. Towner says in the introduction:

> From these indentures can be learned something about the ethnic background of Boston's poor in the eighteenth century, the kinds of trades that were open to poor children, the extent to which Boston supplied a colony- or state-wide labor market, and the kinds of persons who were willing to take poor boys and girls into their farms, homes, and shops. They provide information for the historian of education, of the family, of the poor, and of the bound labor system. They also provide a starting point for the student of specific trades in eighteenth-century Massachusetts as well as rich genealogical material for researchers in family history.

What is most interesting about these apprenticeships is that the people with whom the child was placed were not all from Boston, nor were they necessarily from Massachusetts. Some of the children were sent to North Yarmouth, Brunswick, Falmouth, Pownalborough, St. Georges, Georgetown, Booth Bay, Fort Pownall, Harpswell, Penobscot, Gouldsborough, Portland, Waldoborough, Machias, Baker Town, Bath, Lincolnville, and Freeport, Maine (which was then a part of Massachusetts); as well as Lebanon, Connecticut; and Chester, Londonderry, and Litchfield, New Hampshire. Some men took on more than one child. George Pynchon, Gent., of Springfield took a fifteen-year-old girl in 1770 and a nine-year-old girl and a seven-year-old boy in 1772. Elijah Williams, Esq., of West Stockbridge took two boys, ages nine and fifteen, and one girl, age seven, in February and July of 1784, consecutively. Between 1788 and 1793, Mr. Thomas Hopkins of Portland took seven children. The list includes the date on which the child was bound out and the date on which the child was freed, usually the eighteenth birthday of the girl and the twenty-first birthday of the boy.

The Boston Overseers of the Poor records, 1733–1925, can be found on microfilm at MHS, NEHGS, and BPL; publishing permission must be obtained from MHS. These records include administrative, financial, and almshouse records, warnings out, letters from the overseers to other towns concerning inhabitants of the almshouse, names of persons receiving relief, and records of the Boston Asylum, as well as a few records of Charlestown and Roxbury before these towns became part of Boston. The Colonial Society is currently working on a transcription of records of the Boston Almshouse from 1735, which are part of the Boston Overseers of the Poor records.

The "Records of admissions and discharges, November 9, 1758–April 27, 1774" lists "3 Children of Akleys" were "sent in" by Captn John Bradford on April 7, 1768. Under "Discharge," it simplys says "Bound out." In Lawrence Towner's published list, Sarah Ackley was bound out to Joshua Clap of Scituate on May 9, 1768; Samuel Ackley was bound out to John Merrill of Topsham on July 23, 1768; and Mary Ackley was bound out to Edward Russel of North Yarmouth on September 6, 1768.

At a meeting of the Selectmen on April 25, 1768, "Mr Paul Farmer Keeper of the Almshouse was directed by two of the Selectmen...to receive into said House, there to be supported at the Province Charge one Elizabeth Hubnocks a poor sick Woman who is not an Inhabitant of any Town in this Province, and has not wherewithall to support himself [sic]." In the "Records of admissions," Eliza Utinocks is listed as being sent in by Captn Saml Partridge on April 20, 1768. She was age forty-six and is listed as having died.

ARCH houses records of many of the nineteenth-century institutions set up to care for the poor, orphaned, ill, or mentally ill. While many of these institutions were located outside of Boston, the following examples show that people with Boston connections were sent to these institutions. For a complete list of these records, see Appendix Seven. Many of the children housed at these institutions were placed out to families and sometimes adopted. Such adoptions will be found in the county probate records. One example of an adoption is the case of Samuel Parkinson, born in Boston on February 22, 1877, son of Lizzie Parkinson (unmarried). The "child was brought in February 1878 to the Temporary Home for the Destitute a charitable institution...in Boston and given up to said institution for the purpose of a adoption." He was adopted by David and Olive Bastian of Clinton, Massachusetts, so the adoption papers are in Worcester County.

"Bailey & Co. Views of Boston, The Blind Asylum, South Boston"
Courtesy of The Bostonian Society / Old State House

One of the earliest of these charitable organizations was the Boston Female Asylum, founded and run by Boston society women, with available records from 1800 to 1867. Many Boston mothers and fathers unable to care for their daughters voluntarily placed them in the Female Asylum. When they did so they had to sign the following statement:

> We the Subscribers solicitors that our children should receive the benefits and advantages of the Boston Female Asylum, and the Board of Managers being willing to receive and provide for, and also place them out in virtuous Families untill the age of Eighteen years, Agreeable to the rules and regulations of the Society, provided we do severally relinguish our children to them, we do hereby promise not to interfere on the management of them in any respect whatever, nor visit them without their consent. And in consideration of their benevolence in the receiving and providing for them, we do relinguish all right and claim to them and their services, untill they shall arrive to Eighteen years of age. And severally engage that we will not ask or receive any conpensation for the same, nor take them from, or induce to leave the Families where they may be placed by the Board of managers of the Asylum.

The Registers of children admitted to the Female Asylum date from 1800 to 1867 and record the age, names and/or birthdates, date of admission, and date and time of placement. Some children were eventually returned to their families. For example, Lucretia Cochran was admitted in October 1853 and given to her mother in April 1854; Catharine Hall was admitted in March 1827 and placed with her grandmother, Mrs. Mary Page, on October 27, 1841; and Mary Jane and Elizabeth Kelley were admitted in April 1844 and were "Permitted to go under the care of Patric Nolan to their father James Kelley of Dublin Ireland - who sent for them" in March 1846.

Children were placed with families both in Boston and without: Clara Kingsbury was admitted in August 1860 and placed out in October 1864 with Mr. and Mrs. B. Howard of West Bridgewater; Susan Rowson was admitted October 26, 1813, and placed out on January 21, 1821, with Mr. and Mrs. Cox of Portland, Maine; and Sarah McIntire was admitted July 31, 1810, and placed out in June 1816 with Eliphalet and Mary Dickenson of Deerfield. Some siblings were split up, as in the case of Arria Sargent Renott and Jane Flagg Renott, who were admitted on March 31, 1812. Arria was placed out in September 1815 with Seth and Ann Terry of Hartford, Connecticut, while Jane was placed out on March 30, 1819, with the Rev. S. Swift and his wife of Nantucket, Massachusetts. Jane Elizabeth and Helen Josephine King were admitted in March 1857, and while Jane was placed out in June 1861 with Mr. & Mrs. N. Smith Jr. of Woodbury, Connecticut, her sister Helen was returned to their mother in November 1862.

A few children died in the Asylum. Rosanna Kenney, admitted in August 1854 at the age of six, died of consumption on January 21, 1857. Grace

McFarlane, who was three when admitted on January 24, 1804, died just a few months later on October 8; no cause of death is listed.

While the information in the above registers is helpful, it is in the minutes of meetings where one will often find stories of why children were placed in the Asylum. Here are several examples:

A child named Caroline Scholtz, was recommended to the notice of the Board....Her situation was thus represented by Mrs. M.L. Smith. Her parents had lived in very comfortable circumstances untill they became impoverished by the extreme intemperance and improvidence of her father. The exertions of her mother, on whom the care of his business and of their numerous family entirely devolved, were their only support. She died during the last winter, leaving seven children to poverty and wretchedness. The charity of friends was exerted in their behalf, and the child for whom admission into the Asylum was not solicited, set to a relative, who herself in indigent circumstances, consented to keep her untill the next August, in consideration of receiving from her father some articles of old furniture as a compensation. At the expiration of the next month she would be thrown on the protection of a grandmother, who, at the advanced age of eighty two years, procured subsistance by keeping a small shop; and who already had the charge of two of these orphan children. These circumstances, and the strength and fervency of the expressions of gratitude, with which this aged and unfortunate woman received information of the probability of her grandchild's admittance into the Asylum, were a very powerful and efficient appeal to the feelings of those, who, unanimously acknowledging the claims of age and poverty of childhood and helplessness.

The mother of Selina Sargent died about two years since, leaving five children to the care of an indigent and intemperate father, who was utterly incapable of performing this duty. The three oldest girls were placed at service in respectable families; the fourth, a boy, is a wretched wanderer about the streets. Selina, the youngest, being, from her extreme youth, incapable of performing the service required in a situation like her sisters', remained with her father, exposed to all the hardships of poverty and all the contagion of vice. The house in which he lived was occupied by other boarders, of similar grade and character to his own. One apartment only was appropriated as the bed-room of the whole, and one bed contained the little Selina and her abandoned father. She has two aunts whose characters render their interposition on her behalf much more to be dreaded than wished. Her father is willing to give her up to this charity, and the yet uncontaminated child may now be saved from the destruction to which her present situation seems so inevitably to lead.

Mrs. Codman said she had on the preceding afternoon received the following account from a young woman whose very apparent wretchedness gave painful testimony to its truth. She has been left a widow with one child; had again married and again became a mother. An illness which prevented her husband from continuing his accustomed employment, brought its usual effect to those whose daily support depends on their daily labour. Unable to raise ten dollars for the payment of a debt he had contracted, he was threatened with imprisonment; to avoid this, though hardly recovered from sickness, he left his family and fled. His wife, deserted and in want, is now in daily expectation of giving birth to another child. For her oldest girl, the orphan child of her former husband, she seeks the protection of this society. The name of the woman is Brown, that of the child, Mary Grant.

State almshouses in Tewksbury and Monson began operating in the second half of the nineteenth century. The available records for the Tewksbury Almshouse are as follows: children's records from 1855 to 1869; inmate case histories 1860 to 1896; and weekly returns of admissions and discharges from 1894 to 1918. People were sent to Tewksbury from all over Massachusetts, and their case histories contain varying amounts of information, as these examples show:

> James Carney, 26, from Boston January 17, 1868, born Ireland Co. Roscommon, laborer, landed in Boston $1^{1/2}$ years ago per the "Delivan," there 6 months, then to Brookline 6 months, no relatives, in no other institution, frozen thumb, discharged February 18, 1868.

> Bridget and Sarah Mulhearn, 33 and 8, from Boston January 18, 1868, born in Ireland Co. Galway, husband Michael dead 2 years, landed Boston 18 years ago, there most of time since, no relatives but sister Mrs. Wm. Boyle in Amesbury - sister-in-law Mrs. Murphy 46 Athens St. South Boston, and Mrs. Rowley in 5th St. South Boston, no other relatives, in no other institution, sprained foot.

> William Thompson, 51, from Boston January 29, 1868, born St. Johnsbury VT, married wife dead, turner, went to Sharon VT when 3, there 14 years, then to Bridgeton VT where father died, enlisted 1842 in Albany in 7th Regt. Infantry served 11 years, enlisted 32d Mass. Co. I July 1862, lost eye at Antietam, then enlisted in 2d Vet. NY Cavalry, served 1 year, then to Hartford VT, came from Keene NH to Lynn 16 days ago, don't know how, wants to go to Keene, lived Attleboro 2 months before enlisting in 32d, in Boston before that, no relations, in no other institutions, bruised chest and face.

The Boston Insane Hospital or Lunatic Hospital (records available from 1855 to 1907), the Hospital at Rainsford Island (1854 to 1866), and the Massachusetts School for Idiotic and Feeble-minded Youth (1864 to 1909) were all located in Boston.

The registers of the Boston Insane Hospital contain name, age, sex, civil condition, birthplace, residence, committed by, committed from, committed on, discharged on, removed by, and remarks for each patient. For example:

> "Wm. E. Foley, age 30, male, born Boston, residence Boston, committed on Jan. 7, 1880, discharged on Feb. 23, 1911, removed by the Board of Insanity, to Medfield Hospital"; and "Maria F. Dennis, age 69, female, widow, born

New Hampshire, residence Boston, admitted by probate court Dec. 7, 1903, died Jan. 3, 1904 from exhaustion of Melancholia."

The Registers of the Hospital at Rainsford Island contain name, age, birthplace, marital status, occupation, previous health, habits, color, date of admission, disease, duration before admission, condition, result, departure, and remarks for each patient. Many of the patients were recent immigrants, such as "John Kerrigan, age 22, born Ireland, married, tailor, poor health, irregular habits, admitted August 19, 1854, Phthises for 1 year, very feeble, not improved, departed October 13, 1854, sent to Ireland"; and "Mary Manning, age 24, born Ireland, married, housewife, good health, admitted April 3, 1855, Parturition for 4 hours, favorable condition, had child April 4, 1855." The Hospital also took in Civil War soldiers, such as "Sergt Wm Griffen, Late of Co. I, 2nd N.H. Vols, Fever and Ague, married to Abigail Brown at R.I. Hospital"; and "Wm Parker late of Co. L, 1st Ky Arty, Loss of Leg, Died August 8th 1865."

The Registers of the Massachusetts School for Idiotic and Feeble-Minded Youth contain name, age, birthplace, when admitted, by whom supported, whether in school or workshop, when when discharged, whether discharged or died, and remarks for each patient. For example: "Harvey Gillette, age 9, born at the Monson Almshouse, was admitted Sept. 9, 1868, supported by the state, was discharged Jan. 23, 1877, found a place to work"; and "Angus Finlayson, age 6, born Nova Scotia, residence Boston, admitted Oct. 20, 1908, supported by the state, in school, died March 20, 1909 from Pneumonia followed by scarlet fever."

Sarah J. Shoenfeld begins her article "Applications and Admissions To The Homes for Aged Colored Women in Boston, 1860–1887" (*NEHGR* 155:251) with this quotation: "It having been ascertained by Mrs. R.P. Clarke that a number of aged colored women now residing in the City of Boston are in a destitute and helpless condition, and it having been suggested by her that an institution should be established for their assistance and support..." As with the records mentioned above, these records contain very interesting stories of women, and Ms. Shoenfeld has added to this information with intensive footnotes.

Mary Robinson (Robertson?). Recommended by Mrs. William Swift and admitted May 19, 1860. She is eighty seven years of age, was born in Slavery in the West Indies and was carried to France in her childhood. During the French Revolution of 1789 she was brought to this country by the exiled family of her mistress. Being left destitute at the death of her mistress she supported her self very respectably as long as her strength lasted, by selling apples in the streets of Boston. During the last thirty years she has been supported by the Catholic Church of which she is a member...

Mrs. Elizabeth Babcock. Applied for admission herself. Recommended by Miss Stone and Rev. Charles Mason – Admitted June 22nd, 1861. She was born in St. Johns, New Brunswick and is now 63 years of age. She has married, and lived in New York until her husband's death – a period of nineteen years. She then came to Boston, and opened a boarding house, and supported herself in this way for nearly twenty years. She is now a sufferer from rheumatism, and unable on this account to support herself any longer. Died 1881.

NEHGS' mansuscript collection contains one volume of "Admissions to Boston City Hospital," covering October 1867 to December 1870. The library possesses two index volumes for the hospital, covering April 1889 to April 1900, but not the volumes to which they refer. The Admissions volume provides admission date, patient name, hospital ward, patient age, marital status, occupation, disease, birthplace, current residence, date of discharge, and treatment results. Most entries are for foreign-born individuals, and only the country of birth is noted.

The reasons for admission vary widely and include frozen feet, stabbed groin, chronic gastritis, and injuries from a fall down stairs. One entry of note depicts a sixteen-year-old admitted for a facial wound, the result of a gunshot. Admitted on April 22, he was released "well" on May 4. A typical example is that of thirty-nine year old G. E. Butledge, admitted to Ward B. on January 6, 1868. Butledge is described as a married cabinet-maker, born in Ireland, and living at 12 LaGrange Street. Diagnosed with stricture urethra, he was subsequently relieved, and discharged on October 3, 1868.

The final page of this volume includes a tally of the 1,584 patients admitted during these three years. The nativity of the patients broke down this way: born in Boston 186, born in other Massachusetts towns 116 , Maine 92, New Hampshire 29, Vermont 10, Connecticut 4, New York 22, middle states 13, southern states 12, western states 4, British Provinces 154, England 80, Ireland 724, Germany 47, Norway 2, Persia 6, Sweden 12, France 11, Scotland 26, Prussia 1, Switzerland 5, Western Islands 5, Denmark 1, Belgium 1, Russia 3, Italy 1, Poland 2, and unknown 20.

6 PROBATE RECORDS

Boston is part of Suffolk County, and probate records, wills, administrations, and guardianships are handled at the county level. The very earliest Suffolk County probate records are published in *Suffolk County Wills, Abstracts of the Earliest Wills Upon Record in the County of Suffolk, Massachusetts, From The New England Historical and Genealogical Register* (Baltimore, 1984). These abstracts should be used with caution because they are very brief and may not contain all the important information.

> The work primarily of William B. Trask, this long series of will abstracts appeared at intervals over a period of forty-five years in *The New England Historical and Genealogical Register*. Initiated by Samuel G. Drake in January 1848, the series was entrusted three years later to Mr. Trask, who continued it without interruption until 1866, then set it aside for ten years, returning to it in 1876 and carrying it forward for another two years. Sixteen years later, in 1894, Walter K. Watkins added the final installments.

> The series embodies abstracts of the earliest wills and inventories of Suffolk County, Massachusetts, representing, in substance, the first thirty years or so of the county's estate records.

For the short period from 1686 to 1689, during the Andros administration, all probated estates for the "Dominion of New England" can be found in Suffolk County probate records.

Suffolk County probate record books and docket indexes are available on microfilm through 1881 at NEHGS and through 1916 at FHL. The more recent records are located at the Registry of Probate in the Suffolk County Courthouse. The dockets, which contain the original papers for each file, have not been microfilmed; these are housed at the MSA through 1894. It is best to utilize both sets of probate records because the docket index lists some documents as "missing," meaning that there is a copy in the record book but the original document is no longer in the docket envelope; or as "no record," meaning that there is an original document in the docket envelope, but no copy was entered into the record books. Receipts, such as those from children acknowledging receipt of their portion of an estate, are almost never entered into the record books, but can be very important to researchers.

At one point, the probate office tried to rectify this discrepancy with a "New Series" of record books, into which were copied documents not entered at the time of the event. In the docket indexes, the volume and page numbers are indicated as being in the New Series. The New Series volumes begin with number 1 and as a result are often confused with the earliest original record books. In fact, by the time the probate record books were microfilmed, some of the volumes were out of order. This was not clear to microfilmers, so the volumes were filmed in the order presented. If you do not find the person you seek on the page indicated in the docket index for an original record book, try looking for the same volume number in the New Series.

Annie Haven Thwing traced the ownership of land in Boston to 1800 and published her findings in *The Crooked and Narrow Streets of Boston* (Boston, 1925). She created brief abstracts of Boston town, land, and probate records on three-by-five cards, known as the "Thwing Collection," housed at MHS. This alphabetical card file is very helpful if you are researching a large Boston family or a family in which first names are repeated. Her cards can help sort out the records of one individual, and can therefore save time when searching for the full record in the probate and land records. This collection is now available on CD from NEHGS.

Before the formation of Norfolk County in 1793, the towns of that county were considered part of Suffolk County. The towns of Chelsea, Revere, and Winthrop still are included with Boston in Suffolk County. The Thwing Collection only abstracts probate records for residents of Boston proper.

Inventories included in most probate files can be helpful in creating a picture of how these residents lived. After about 1840, personal estate is generally lumped together and given just one appraisal amount. Amasa Davis, probably my most illustrious ancestor, died in 1825, leaving a "Mansion House" on Washington Street (see p. 119). He owned four other properties; these five properties were together valued at $45,000. The Mansion House inventory of was done room-by-room (see Appendix Five). In the Front Parlour was "1 Portrait of the Deceased," painted by Gilbert Stuart; in the Cellar was "1 Silver Sugar Bowl," probably the one made by Paul Revere and passed to my grandfather, who sold it to a museum. Note in the inventory the backgammon board, an umbrella, waffle iron, and bottles of catsup in the cellar.

The inventory gives some idea of how Amasa lived. For example, the number of chairs he owned indicates that he must have done quite a lot of entertaining: twelve "fancy chairs" in the Front Parlour, another twelve "fancy chairs" in the Dining Room, fifteen chairs in the Middle Upper Chamber, and six chairs in the Front Chamber. Amasa was chosen Quartermaster General of Massachusetts in 1787, and was elected Captain of the Ancient and Honorable Artillery Company in 1795. His inventory reflects these achievements, with two military hats valued at $1, one sword and pistols at $10, and military clothes at $10.

"House of Amasa Davis"
Courtesy of The Bostonian Society / Old State House

7 LAND RECORDS

The first fourteen volumes of Suffolk County land records from 1629 to 1697 are published. In addition to grantor and grantee indexes, these volumes include indexes of others mentioned in the deeds, such as witnesses, owners of land that borders the property, etc. The later land records and corresponding grantor and grantee indexes to 1885 are on microfilm at NEHGS; FHL has the land records to 1885 and the indexes to 1920. The more recent land records are still at the Registry of Deeds in the Suffolk County Courthouse.

There is also an index to other people mentioned in land records for the period of 1629 to 1799. This index is extremely useful for finding those who may not appear often, or at all, as grantors or grantees. In researching Paix Cazneau, I found Paase Cusenoe once as a grantee and his wife Margaret Casno once as a grantee, but this index led me to two deeds in which the land was bounded by land "formerly granted to Paco Casno" and "land belonging to the heirs of Paco Casno," both dated after his death.

One unusual feature of the Suffolk County grantee–grantor indexes is that brief descriptions of the land are given, in addition to the names, dates, volumes, and page numbers. This is helpful, since towns other than Boston have been or still are part of Suffolk County. Prior to 1793, Suffolk County included those towns now in Norfolk County. Until 1803, Hingham and Hull were part of Suffolk County. Chelsea, Revere, and Winthrop still are in Suffolk County. These land descriptions can help the researcher identify deeds pertaining to John Brown of Boston as significant and separate from John Brown of Hingham or Chelsea. The descriptions might also include comments like "Int[erest] in dower of Sarah Bradshaw in Est[ate] of John Bradshaw"; "Hingham Highway near the Meeting house towards the Burying Place"; "Int[erest] in Est[ate] Edward Tyng"; "Boston Milk St. – Long Lane"; and "Boston Middle St. & Beer Lane."

In Massachusetts, land was granted to the town, and then was granted by the town in lots to settlers. All available land was not necessarily granted at the beginning; there may have been several instances in which lots were laid out to the inhabitants. These grants do not appear in the county land records at the courthouse, but when the land was sold those deeds were recorded in the county. Volume 2 of the Record Commissioners Reports includes the Book of Possessions, which lists the lots of land owned by settlers in 1645. As Robert Charles Anderson explains in "Focus on Boston," *Great Migration Newsletter* (3:3), the lots of land in the Book of Possession are the only ones they owned on Boston neck; the Book of Possession does not include the land they may have been granted off the neck, such as Muddy River (now Brookline), where they pastured their cattle.

As mentioned previously under Probate Records, Annie Haven Thwing traced the ownership of land in Boston to 1800 by briefly abstracting the land, probate, and town records. These records at MHS are known as the "Thwing Collection" and are now available on CD, published by NEHGS. As there may be more than one man of the same name at the same time in Boston, this collection is extremely useful in sorting out those deeds that pertain to the person you are researching.

8 Court Records

The General Court was the highest court for the Massachusetts Bay Colony until 1685, at which time it was reorganized as the Superior Court of Judicature, which functioned until 1780. A later reorganization made the highest court the Supreme Judicial Court, as it is today. These courts were primarily appellate courts covering the entire colony (which included Maine until 1820), but they did have original jurisdiction over some types of cases, such as murder. Minute books of these courts offer brief listings of each case considered at each term. The earliest records are included in Nathaniel B. Shurtleff's *Records of the Governor and Company of the Massachusetts Bay in New England, 1628–1686*, 5 volumes in 6 (Boston, 1853–1854). The Colonial Society of Massachusetts published *Law in Colonial Massachusetts, 1630–1800* (Boston, 1894). Two articles in this volume explain the court system: Michael S. Hindus, "A Guide to the Court Records of Early Massachusetts," and Catherine S. Menand, "A 'magistracy fit and necessary': A Guide to the Massachusetts Court System." The court records to the mid-1800s are now at the Judicial Archives at ARCH.

The Colonial Society of Massachusetts has published the "Records of the Suffolk County Court, 1671–1680" (Collections, volumes 29 and 30). The records of the Court of Assistants for the seventeenth century are published in three volumes called *Records of the Court Assistants of the Colony of Massachusetts Bay* (Boston, 1901–1928). N. B. Shurtleff published in six volumes, *Records of the Governor and Company of Massachusetts Bay in New England 1628–1686* (New York, 1971). Boston residents may also be found in the six volumes of *Province and Court Records of Maine*, published by the Maine Historical Society.

Records of the Supreme Judicial Court from 1686 to 1870 are at the ARCH and FHL. Included in these records are *Volumes of Partitions and Executions from 1694 to 1856*. These contain cases such as court orders to partition an estate. For example, on June 9, 1738, George Partridge of Duxbury, "guardian to minors James Bradford, Zadok Bradford, Eliphalet Bradford, and William Bradford, sons of William Bradford and grandsons of John Bradford, that whereas John Bradford made a deed of gift of land to his grandsons, allowing John and his wife to live on the land during their lives, and now that John is deceased," is petitioning for an order to divide the land between the four minor children and their grandmother. The court agreed and appointed three men to make the division.

Also included in these records are those pertaining to probate matters from 1760 to 1870. When heirs challenged a will or some other aspect of probating an estate, the case was appealed to the Supreme Judicial Court. For example, Rachel and Samuel Dwight presented a last will and testament for Michael Dwight, late of Dedham, and it was accepted by the probate judge. Anna Lyon contested the will, saying that Michael "long before the making of the said supposed Will, and at that time was by age debilitated in his Understanding," and was "unknowing of the Contents of the said supposed Will." Rachel and Samuel answered that Michael "at the time of his making said Will was of sound and disposing mind, and well knew the Contents of it." The court agreed with the probate judge and the will stood.

The records of the Court of Admiralty, which handled maritime matters under the jurisdiction of the British Crown, are from 1718 to 1772.

Besides the minute books, there are also file papers for each of these courts — including writs, petitions, depositions, accounts, etc. — which until 1883 were just loose papers. Between 1883 and 1907, John Noble, Clerk of the Supreme Judicial Court, supervised the sorting and indexing of these loose papers into large volumes now known as the Suffolk Files, a very important set of court records on microfilm at ARCH and FHL.

The Suffolk Files are indexed with several sets of indexes that can be a bit intimidating but are well worth the trouble. Basic writs for debt or trespass are indexed with just surnames, such as Brown vs. Jones. Other records, such as petitions, depositions, accounts, etc., are indexed by full names. This collection also includes many copies of warnings out submitted by towns, including Boston. Warnings out did not necessarily mean that the recipient had to leave town. The recipient of such a warning was given to understand that, should the need arise, the town would not provide assistance or assume responsibility for the welfare of the individual in question. For more information on warnings out, consult Josiah Henry Benton, *Warning Out in New England, 1656–1817* (Boston, 1911: reprint 1992).

The following list of people included in just one Boston warning out serves to show that people came to Boston from many different places:

On May 1, 1765, the Selectmen issued a warrant to Robert Love to warn out several people. The warnings generally give the date they came to Boston and with whom they are living.

On May 2 he warned John Means who came from Framingham.

On May 4 he warned Abagail Hastings who came from Littleton.

On May 11 he warned Sarah Field who came from "Brantry" and John May who came from Philadelphia.

On May 15 he warned Sarah Montcrieff who came from Roxbury.

On May 16 he warned Anna Salter who came from Stoughton.

On May 17 he warned Mary Allair who came from Charlestown.

On May 18 he warned Daniel Moor, his wife Abigail, sons Joshua, Daniel, and Joseph, and daughter Lucretia, who came from Annapolis Royal and John Lyn who came from New York.

On May 21 he warned Mary [Donnilson?] who came from New Castle upon Delaware River in "Pensilvania," Susannah Cain who came from St. Georges at Eastward, and Mary Jackson who came from Marblehead.

On May 24 he warned John Hunter, Daniel Caley, and Alexander Cummings who came from Londonderry, New Hampshire, Joseph Dun who came from Lancaster in Pensilvania, and Anna Bill who came from Chelsea.

On May 27 he warned Edward Cumberford who came from Georgetown at the Eastward.

Under the above courts in each county were the courts of Common Pleas, which heard civil cases, and the courts of General Sessions, which heard criminal cases. Alicia C. Williams abstracted the minute books of the Suffolk County Court of Common Pleas from January 1701 to October 1708 in *The Mayflower Descendant* Volumes 35 to 44. The records for the Court of Common Pleas from 1701 to 1855 are on microfilm or microfiche at the BPL and FHL; those from 1701 to 1737 are at ARCH, and are generally indexed by plaintiff only. These cases often refer to settlement of estates and can include helpful information, such as, "John Barrell, Boston, cooper and Abiah his wife who was formerly relict widow and still is executrix of the will of George Beard, late Boston, marriner decd," or "Johanna Callender, daughter and only child of George Callender, late Boston, marriner, deced, an infant, by Thomas Child, Boston, painter and Katherine his wife her guardians VS the estate of George Callender."

There are four volumes for the Suffolk County Court of General Sessions 1702 to 1780 at ARCH and FHL. Apprenticeships were primarily private arrangements, but if trouble occurred it might make the court records, as these examples show:

Upon hearing the Petition of John Valentine Koppler Complaining against his Master John Brand of Boston for Severe and immoderate beating him &c and the said John Brands answer thereto – Ordered That the said John Koppler forthwith return to the Service of his said Master John Brand upon the said Brands giving Caution by Recoginzance to the Queen in the Sum of Ten pounds That he will Treat his said Servant according to his Indenture and use no Cruelty to him.

Samuel Ranger of Boston Taylor being Complained of for evil Intreating his Servant or Apprentice named William Russell Son of Thomas Russell deced and being heard thereon; Ordered That the said William Russell be dismissed from the Service of his said Master Saml Ranger; Joseph Russell of Boston aforesaid Shopkeeper Uncle of the said William Russell engaging to See him well disposed of in Service.

The General Sessions also include cases dealing with a variety of criminal activity, such as drunkenness, stealing, receiving stolen goods, and having a child out of wedlock:

Katharine Horton of Brookline Singlewoman being present by the Grand Jury for having a bastard Child by Negro Coffee Servant to Peter Boylston of Brookline...Appeared and Owned the same and that it is a Boy now living – Ordered That the said Katharine Horton shall be Whipped Twenty Stripes at the publick Whipping post and be Obliged to maintain her Child; but if She be unable so to do, then to be disposed of in Service for that end.

9 CITY DIRECTORIES

In 1789, Boston, following the example of Philadelphia and New York, published its first city directory, a listing of the business community. The title page says "A List of the MERCHANTS, MECHANICS, TRADERS, and others, of the Town of BOSTON; in Order to enable Strangers to find the Residence of any Person."

The listings were very brief: John Crosby, shop-keeper, No. 39 Newbury-street; John Jenkins, baker, Union-street; Nehemiah Whitmarsh, wharfinger, house in Eliot's-street, wharf south end. The first entry is simply, Samuel Adams, Hon. Winter-street. While most of the entries are for men, some women, such as Mary Gray, milliner, Hanover-street, are included.

Some features of this directory were carried on in later directories, such as a map of the town with street names; lists of Public Offices, Acting Justices, Barristers at Law, Attorneys at Law, Physicians and Surgeons; and lists of members of the Fire Companies. By 1836, the city directory contained many lists, such as United States Officers, Commonwealth Officers, Constables, Nurses, Undertakers, Banks, Charitable Societies, Churches and Ministers, Arrival and Departure of Stages, and Hotels and Taverns.

The Boston city directories are on microfiche at NEHGS and FHL and on microfilm at BPL through 1981.

City directories can help you trace a family as it moves around town. In the nineteenth century, many people living in cities never owned land or homes, but lived in a series of boardinghouses or hotels. You may find a family moving every year. With a common name such as John Murphy, a particular occupation like baker, rather than just laborer, may help track a certain family.

City directories may also help to determine the ward in which a family lived, and this may help in finding a family in one of the Federal or State censuses. Remember though, that the information for a directory was collected the year before publication or very early in the directory year, so check the 1911 directory as well as in the 1910 directory, for where a person may have been living in the 1910 census.

City directories may also help you find other members of a family. As sons came of age or started working, they may have been listed as boarders at the same address as the father. Also, the first listing of a person may help determine when he or she came to Boston. By the twentieth century, the Boston directories often list the death date of a person in the directory for the year following the death. When someone left town, the directory generally indicated the town to which they moved. The 1910 city directory for the surname Murphy included the following:

Murphy, Dominick, removed to Cambridge

Murphy, Edward J., died January 6, 1910

Murphy, John, of 14 Everett, Charlestown, died January 10, 1910

Murphy, John J., of 95 Calumet, Dorchester, died May 26, 1909

Murphy, John P., of 260 E. Cottage, Dorchester, removed to Canton

Murphy, John T., of 395 E. Fifth, South Boston, died August 12, 1909

Murphy, Leo M., died May 12, 1909

Murphy, Patrick J., of 672 E. Second, South Boston, removed to Bristol NH

Murphy, Thomas, of 7 Stafford, Roxbury, died July 23, 1909

Murphy, Thomas J., of 264 Norfolk Ave., Roxbury, died November 2, 1909

Murphy, Timothy J., of 26 Bailey, Dorchester, died March 5, 1910

City directories usually include many business advertisements and an index to the advertisors. Be sure to check in the front or back of the directory for a list of those people who were too late to be included in the general listing.

John Haven Dexter was very interested in Boston families in the early-nineteenth century. An early member of the New England Historic Genealogical Society, NEHGS owns several of his manuscripts. His first manuscript to be published was *First Boston City Directory (1789) Including Extensive Annotations by John Haven Dexter (1791–1876)* (Ann S. Lainhart, NEHGS, 1989), also published in *The New England Historical and Genealogical Register*, 140:23–62, 138–170, 230–263, 321–330. Dexter collected information on those listed in the first city directory from many sources, including his own firsthand knowledge. While not error free, this information can add valuable details about a family. NEHGS also published another volume of his collection, though this one is not tied directly to the 1789 city directory: *John Haven Dexter's Memoranda of the Town of Boston in the 18th & 19th Centuries* (Robert J. Dunkle and Ann S. Lainhart, 1997).

10 MILITARY RECORDS AND SEAMAN'S RECORDS

In records such as vital and town records, men may be called Sergeant, Lietuenant, or Captain. These titles indicated that the men were in the local militia, though Captain could also refer to sea captains. There are several groups of military records for Massachusetts that include Boston men, beginning at ARCH with the "Massachusetts Archives" (or "Felt Collection"), one section of which contains military records from 1643 to 1775. In the card catalog, there are drawers labeled for military records.

For the colonial period, there are original records at ARCH, George M. Bodge's *Soldiers in King Phillip's War* (1896; reprint 1967), and the following four volumes, all published by NEHGS and the Society of Colonial Wars in the Commonwealth of Massachusetts:

> Myron O. Stachiw, *Massachusetts Officers and Soldiers, 1723–1743, Dummer's War to the War of Jenkins' Ear.*

> Robert E. MacKay, *Massachusetts Soldiers in the French and Indian Wars, 1744–1755.*

> Nancy S. Voye, *Massachusetts Officers in the French and Indian Wars, 1748–1763.*

> K. David Goss and David Zarowin, *Massachusetts Officers and Soldiers in the French and Indian Wars, 1755–1756.*

For information on the Revolutionary War, there is the seventeen-volume set, *Massachusetts Soldiers and Sailors of the Revolutionary War.* The ARCH has additional information on Revolutionary soldiers found after publication. This addendum can be found on microfilm at ARCH and NEHGS. NARA has the "General Index to Compiled Military Service Records of Revolutionary War Soldiers" and the pension records for Revolutionary War soldiers. Abstracts of these pensions were published in Virgil D. White's *Genealogical Abstracts of Revolutionary War Pension Files,* 4 volumes.

For the War of 1812, consult *Records of the Massachusetts Volunteer Militia*

Called Out by the Governor of Massachusetts to Suppress a Threatened Invasion during the War of 1812–14 (Boston, 1913), and at NARA, the pension index for veterans of the War of 1812. The diary of William Ingersoll Champney of Boston can be found on the NEHGS website. Champney worked for Isaiah Thomas for a few months in 1814, and his diary provides a first person account of Boston during the War of 1812.

For the Civil War, there is the eight-volume set, Massachusetts in the Army and Navy during the War of 1861-65 (Boston, 1931-1935). At NARA there is an index to pension applications submitted between 1861 and 1934 for military service performed up to 1916, as well as indexes to compiled service records of volunteer Union soldiers from each New England state. ARCH has a free booklet "Collections of the Massachusetts Archives Civil War Records" that lists all the various series that have material from the 1861 to 1865 period. Included in these is "List of seamen and officers from Boston in the U.S. Navy (1861-1865)" and the "Rainsford Island Hospital register (1854-1866)." Rainsford Island is in the Boston harbor and the administration of the hospital shifted repeatedly between the city of Boston and the Commonwealth of Massachusetts. Many of the collections have material organized by town and may then have material on Boston inhabitants.

The NARA has abstracts of service records of naval officers for the period 1798 to 1893.

The draft cards for World War I are on microfilm at NARA. The cards for Boston are alphabetical within each draft board. Most of the draft board numbers correspond to the twelve ward numbers, but wards three and four are in draft board three and ward five in is draft boards four and five. These cards are very likely to give specific information on birth place of the foreign-born. For example, James P. Casey was born in Dunmore, Ireland on April 15, 1894, and Angelo Cappuccia was born in Mirabella, Cavellino, Italy on December 2, 1886. Other available information includes age, residence, citizenship status, occupation, employer, dependents, and a brief physical description.

Most of the draft cards for World War II are still covered by a privacy period, but those of the fourth draft, which was taken in 1942 and included men born between 1877 and 1897, are open. NARA has cards for Connecticut, New Hampshire, Rhode Island, and Vermont. They are working on the cards for Massachusetts; those cards should be available soon.

Original military records for Massachusetts from 1776 to 1940 are available at Commonwealth of Massachusetts – Military Division – History Research and Museum. They have records in the following categories: Early militia (1776–1819), Massachusetts militia (1820–1839), pre-Civil War (1840–1860),

Image of Long Wharf
Courtesy of The Bostonian Society / Old State House

Civil War (1861–1865), Reconstruction (1866–1897), Spanish-American War/Philippines Insurrection (1898–1916), World War I (1917–1919) including State Guard records, and National Guard (1920–1940).

The crew's lists recorded at the Custom House in Boston are at NARA. These lists are sporadic from 1867 through 1884, and complete from January 1891 through May 1918. They are arranged chronologically and have the name of the ship on the outside of the folded list. On October 6, 1880, "W.L. Staples, Master of the said Sch. *W.E. Palmer* do solemnly, sincerely, and truly swear that the within List contains the names of all the Crew of the said Sch., together with the places of their births and residence, as far as I can ascertain." The *Walter E. Palmer* was out of Stockton, Maine, on its way to "Hayti." The crew consisted of W.L. Staples, born Maine, age fifty-four, 5'11" in height, and light complexion; T.W. Spearwater, born Massachusetts, forty, 5'9", and light complexion; Joseph Frank, born Portugal, age twenty-seven, 5'8", and dark complexion; August Norden, born Norway, twenty-two, 5'11", and dark complexion; John Nyston, born Norway, twenty-six, 5'8", and light complexion; and Kris Nixson, born Norway, twenty-two, 5'8", and dark complexion. In later years the form also asks for their "capacity," or job on board ship, and for the color of their eyes and hair.

The Seaman's Protection Papers, or Applications for Seaman's Certificate of American Citizenship, can be found at NARA from 1918 through 1938 and have a wealth of information. They contain pictures of the seamen and the collection is fully indexed as well. A typical example is John L. Nolan, who was issued a certificate on June 24, 1918. He was born in Boston on October 15, 1891, graduated from Technology Marine Engineering School, and was a resident of 197 Jefferson Ave., Salem, Massachusetts. He was age twenty-six, was 5' 9" in height, weighed 135 pounds and had brown eyes and hair and a dark complexion. Included with his application is an abstract birth certificate from the City of Boston showing that John L. Nolan was born on October 15, 1891, the son of John and Allie.

NARA also has Citizen Seaman's Identification Cards. It was "unlawful for a citizen seaman to sail in a vessel from any United States port or to land from any vessel in any such port unless in possession of this card." These cards also include pictures of the seamen. A typical example is John Mulvey who was issued a card in 1920. He was born in Boston to parents who were both born in Ireland; he was age twenty-nine on October 29, 1920, 5'10" in height; fair complexion, brown hair, blue eyes, and had a scar on the palm of his left hand. These cards also have an index by name.

On the NEHGS website is a new database of the Boston Sea Fencibles' Signal Roll, based on material at NEHGS. The Boston Sea Fencibles was chartered June 13, 1817, by the Massachusets legislature. This organization was formed as a naval militia to serve the Commonwealth when needed. Membership was open to those over the age of twenty-one who had commanded a vessel on a foreign voyage or had served as first mate or supercargo on a foreign voyage.

11 TAX LISTS

Volume 1 of the Boston Record Commissioners Reports contains seventeenth-century tax lists. Boston is included in *The Massachusetts Tax Valuation List of 1771*, Bettye Hobbs Priutt (Boston, 1978). Some of the manuscript pages of the 1771 valuation list were destroyed before publication, so not all Massachusetts and Maine towns are represented in Priutt's book.

The Rare Book Room at the BPL has tax lists, "taking books" kept by the town assessors, and valuation lists from 1780 to 1820, but not for every year. The "Assessors' 'Taking Books' of the Town of Boston, 1780" was published in *The Bostonian Society Publications*, 9:9. It includes the name of the head of household; the number of polls in the household; a column named "Rents" that probably indicates amounts in pounds, shillings, and pence; and the occupation of the head of household. Polls were men over sixteen who owned enough property to be taxed. For example, my fifth great-grandfather, Amasa Davis, Trader, is listed with one poll and £150.

The 1798 Direct Tax, published in volume 22 of the Record Commissioners Reports and available on NEHGS' website, *www.NewEnglandAncestors.org*, includes information on land owners in Boston with brief descriptions of the land and buildings. It is also a substitute for the missing 1800 Federal census.

Lewis Bunker Rohrbach has reprinted *Boston Taxpayers in 1821* with a full name index (Camden, ME, 1988). The columns in this book include the names of the taxpayers, the ward and street where they lived, the valuation of the their real and personal estate, the number of polls, their state, town and county tax, abatements, the amount of the tax, and the owner of the real estate. Again, my fifth great-grandfather, Amasa Davis, is listed under his name with five pieces of property on Washington Street in Ward twelve; the total land value was £4700; personal estate value was £6000 ; his state tax was £10-84-0, and his town and county tax was £75-29-0 shillings, for a total tax of £86-13-0. He also owned one other piece of land on Washington Street rented to Williams & Viles; two pieces on Orange Street rented to Aaron Chapin and Luther Felton; and one piece on Middle Street rented to Theodore Dexter.

There is a database on the NEHGS website for a Boston tax list in 1831 which contains the names of the taxpayers, the ward in which they lived, the value of their real estate, tax paid on real estate, value of personal estate, and the tax paid on the personal estate.

Tax Valuation Records from 1822 to 1895 and 1945 to 1973 are at BCA. Those from 1896 to 1944 are available at the Research Library Division of the BPL.

12 BUSINESS PAPERS, ACCOUNT BOOKS, AND DIARIES

Many, if not most, of the Boston area repositories have manuscript collections that may include business papers, account books, or diaries for Boston residents. These can be accessed through H. Forbes' *New England Diaries, 1602–1800, A Descriptive Catalog of Diaries, Orderly Books, and Sea Journals* (1967); W. Matthews' *American Diaries Written Prior to 1861* (1959); *American Diaries in Manuscript, 1580–1954* (1974); and *The National Union Catalog of Manuscript Collections;* and *Guide to the Manuscript Collections of the New England Historic Genealogical Society* (2002). The list of diaries owned by NEHGS is available on their website, and the diaries of Jeremiah Bumstead and "Boyle's Occurances," both published in the *Register*, now are available on the website. The 1744–1746 diary of Jonathan Willis, housewright, of Boston, is being transcribed by D. Brenton Simons for publication in the *Register*.

Boston has been home for businesses almost from the very beginning. The business papers and account books of many of these businessmen are at the MHS, the Baker Library at Harvard, and several of the other repositories in the Boston area. One such man was Caleb Davis, the brother of my fifth great-grandfather. The following, from "Caleb Davis, and His Funeral Dinner" (*Proceedings of the Massachusetts Historical Society*, March 1921) describes his business history:

> We know that in 1759 he was a partner with his uncle, Robert Pierpont, in a retail provision and grocery business, soon after setting up a store of his own on Orange, now Washington Street....Considerable purchases of rum from Thomas Amory and others are noted. Still later, during part of and after the Revolution, he was a merchant and ship owner in the coastwise, West India, and European trade. After his marriage to...Eleanor Cheever, he was active in the management of a sugar refinery which the Cheevers had owned and carried on for at least fifty years. William Downes Cheever, father-in-law of Caleb Davis, about 1760 calls it the sugar *baking* business. In the Directory for 1796 Davis appears as sugar *refiner*.

In the Caleb Davis Papers at MHS, for the second half of 1759, his accounts show that he imported tea, pimentos, nutmegs, sugar, raisins, brimstone, flour, redwood, and paper. On August 5, 1762, he made an agreement with Joshua Pierpoint: "Recvd of Caleb Davis on Board the Schooner Nancy, Candles Turpintine & Tarr amountg To Nineteen pounds Fiveteen shillings & 1d Lawful money which I am To Sell in the west Indies and Return the [?] in Such Goods as I Shall think Best. The Danger of the Seas & Emeny Excepted Upon Condition of which we are to Share Equally In the Profit in Sale & Returns."

Caleb was very involved in public affairs and the Revolutionary War, as shown by several letters in his collection. On February 11, 1778, Paul Revere wrote him:

> Sir
>
> Yesterday Col Crofts Capt Todd & myself delivered Genl Hancock a Petition from the Officers of our Regiment to lay before the Court. I beg your influence in favor of it...Within the Course of the last year, there has a Major, four Capt, & 10 Subalterns, got their discharge from the Regt, the most of them because they could not maintain them selves and those that are left, are mostly Tradesmen, I fear very much, that if the Court should not grant the prayer of the petition, most of the Officers will leave (all that are good for anything), not out of spleen, but for necesicty. I do asure you there is not an Officer in the Regimt, that has a Coat fitt to wear, I mean a Regimental one. One third of the Regiment is allway on the Out Posts which is as expensive as to be at the Grand Army & no Men do more duty...

Later that year Elijah Caswell of Rochester wrote Caleb "Requesting of you To Send me a few Lines as I might know whether you have Heard any thing from my Son John a prisoner at Halafax." And on June 15, 1779, Willis Hall of Sutton wrote:

> Sir
>
> I am Informed that you are Agent for the Hazzard and whereas my Son Willis Hall Junr was in Boston about ten Days Before Said Hazzard Saled and Since that time I cannot here any thing from him but Suspect he is gon a Privat tearing. I should take it as a Great favour if you would be so good as to Send me word if he the Said Willis Hall Junr name is in the List of the Crew gon in the Vessell above sd and you will Greatly oblidge your Humble Sert.

A letter to Caleb from Sam Adams in Philadelphia ends with this P.S.: "I shall be most obliged if you will write to me when you have Leisure. I wish to know the particular State of publick Affairs in Massachusetts Bay."

After Caleb Davis died in July 1797, a funeral dinner was held and the bill for this dinner was preserved in the family and was published in 1921 by his descendant Frederick Cheever Shattuck. The dinner was held at his house and six dozen chairs were rented; it appears that over 100 men attended this dinner. Ten servants were hired to attend at the table and three cooks and four servants to do the cooking.... The list of food is amazing:

"Beef, fowls, fish & oysters, green peas, onions, lemons & Seville oranges, 25 lb. Potatoes, 4 jars French Cocumbers, 5 jars French Oil, 6 lb. French Bacon, 8 lb. Spanish Bacon, 3 Hams with 22 ½ lb., 25 lb. Flour, 12 lb. Sugar, 150 eggs, 1 fish's tail, 12 lb. Apples, 2 Dozen oranges, cinnamon, anchovies & capers, 2 lb. Sweetmeats for Cakes, 9 pints milk, Salt & Coals, 45 lb. Butter, 2 lb. Hogs Lard, Fruit, Cheese, Raisins, Fruit preserved in Brandy, Biscuits, 3 Bottles Liquor, Caffee & Milk, 7 ¾ lb. Superfine Sugar, 6 lb. Sirop, 6 Bottles Rum, 24 Pajarete Wine, 18 Bottles Malaga, 30 Bottles Sherry, 36 Bottles Bourdeaux, 6 Bottle Peralta, 2 Bottles Frontignanc, 4 Bottles Red Wine, 2 Bottles White Wine, 42 Bottles Beer, and Gin & Brandy."

Frederick Shattuck figured that total bill in 1921 money would be between five and ten thousand dollars. Imagine what it would cost today!

13 CENSUSES

The 1800 federal census for Boston is missing; a part of Suffolk County exists, but nothing for Boston. The 1798 Direct Tax, published as Volume twenty-two of the Record Commissioners Reports can be used as a substitute. Otherwise, Boston is complete for all the federal censuses and the Massachusetts state censuses of 1855 and 1865. At ARCH are the state copies of the 1850, 1860, 1870, and 1880 Federal censuses. Only the 1880 census is microfilmed, but the original volumes can be used when something on the microfilm of the Federal copy is unclear or illegible.

The 1860 federal census for Ward 1 of Boston includes county or town of birth, instead of just the country or state which is more common. Appendix Six is an article on the special features and flaws of this enumeration. It is reprinted with permission of the author Melinde Lutz Sanborn and the *New England Historical and Genealogical Register* (142:25-28).

The City of Boston also took several city censuses and these are found at the BCA. The 1820 city census has the greatest number of columns, to be filled in, as seen below, but only wards 5, 9, 11, and 12 have been found.

1820 BOSTON [CITY] CENSUS

Headings: NAMES; Polls rateable, sixteen years old and upwards, to twenty-one years; Polls rateable, twenty-one years and upwards; Male Polls not rateable, nor supported by the town; Dwelling Houses; Shops within, or adjoining to Dwelling Houses; Other Shops; Distil Houses; Sugar Houses; Ware House, or Stores; Rope Walks; Iron Works and Furnaces; Glass Factories; Bake Houses; Barns or Stables; Buildings and Edifices of the value of $20 & upwards; Superficial feet of Wharf; Tons of Vessels; The amount of Stock in Trade, and Public Securities of every kind; Ounces of Plate; Acres of Tillage Land and Orcharding; Acres of Salt Marsh; Acres of Pasturage; Acres of Land owned by the Town; Horses, three years old and upwards; Oxen, four years old and upwards; Steers and Cows, three years old and upwards; Swine, six months old and upwards; Estates Doomed.

Some examples:

Ward 12, Otis Pope, 1 Barns or Stables, 6 horses

Isaac Vose, 3 polls 16-21, 1 poll over 21; 1 dwelling house, 1 barn or stable, 1 horse, 1 steer or cow

Henry B. Curtis, 10080 feet of wharf, 4 horses

Josiah Knapp, 1 Distil House, 1 Barn or stable; 2 steers or cows

Other censuses at BCA were taken in 1835, 1837, 1840, 1850, and 1855. These censuses have only the names of the head of household, or in some cases only the names of voters, and sex and age categories for the rest of the household. The censuses of 1840 and 1850 are not city copies of the Federal censuses and the 1855 census is not the same as the state census.

Pasted into one 1855 volume is the following instructions for the enumerators:

1. Before calling at the door state in your book the street & section of the street.

2. When calling always state the object of your visit & step into the entry or room & put your book on a table if possible.

3. Ask for the head of the family & never receive information from a doubtful source.

4. After stating in the book it is well to read it to the person & be sure it is all correct.

5. Take all members of the family whether at home or absent.

6. Take boarders & domestics, but not visitors.

7. Put but one family on a line – where there are more than one family in a house, include them in a brace.

8. In all cases be very particular to make a memorandum of all unsettled questions & where the family is absent make a note.

9. Date your return.

10. Persons temporarily absent on business, or at colleges or schools are to be enumerated.

11. State paupers, convicts in Jail, or House of Correction, or inmates of Hospitals, Scholars & student are not to be enumerated if they do not belong to Boston.

12. Children of Foreign parents are to be enumerated among the foreign population.

Qualifications of Voters

Must be 21 years old, have resided in the State 1 year, & in the City 6 months from the 1st of May & have paid a tax assessed within 2 years, & if a Foreigener must have taken out both papers. Take the names in full & be particular & get all – especially the naturalized ones.

Militia

Take all the males Americans & naturalized foreigners from 18 to 45.

There are also state censuses for Boston taken in 1855 and 1865. The original enumerations are at ARCH; microfilm copies are available at NEHGS and FHL. The 1865 state census has two extra features not found this early in the Federal censuses. The first is a column that asks whether the person is single, married, or divorced. The second is a column that asks whether the adult men are legal citizens or naturalized citizens. Available on the NEHGS website is my database of "People of Color in the Massachusetts State Census, 1855–1865," culled from these two state censuses. Boston had a large population of people of color.

14 VOTERS' LISTS

At the BCA there are nineteenth- and early twentieth-century lists of voters arranged by ward. For those non-native-born voters, the lists contain information about how they became voters; whether by their own naturalization or by that of their father. These lists also give the date and court in which the naturalization took place. The lists for male voters begin in 1857 and for those lists from 1857 to 1900 there are five indexes:

> Index of Naturalized Voters, from 1857 to 1878; Registrars of Voters. Surname, first name, book, page number
>
> Index to Naturalized Voters, 1878 to 1888, Board of Election Commissioners. as above
>
> Index To Naturalized Voters, May 1, 1888 To May 1, 1892, Board of Election Commissioners. as above
>
> Index To Naturalized Voters, May 1, 1892 To May 1, 1896, Registrars of Voters. as above
>
> Index to Naturalized Voters, 1896 to 1900, Board of Election Commissioners. Surname, first name, address, ward, precinct, book, page number

SOME EXAMPLES

Register of Naturalized Male Voters, Ward 2, 31 Oct 1864 to 2 Nov 1872

Headings: Date, Name, Signature, [Date] Naturalized, Occupation, Residence, Remarks, Result.

Oct 12, 1868, James F. Cotter, James F. Cotter, by Father Daniel Dec 31, 1852, laborer, Osborn pl.

Oct 19, 1868, Bonheim Kahn, Leavenworth, Kansas, Mar 23, 1861, Porter, Parks 760

Oct 28, 1868, Wm. Mullaby, William Mullaby, says he recd his final papers 28 years ago - burnt - 58 years old, tailor, 57 Billerica, reads very well

Oct 23, 1869, Daniel Leahey, cannot write his name on account of palsy which he contracted in the U.S. Service could write well previous to 1861, Aug 18, 1869, laborer, 34 Clark

Ward 25, No. 36, Register of Voters (Naturalized); alphabetical by first letter of surname.

Headings: Date; Ward; Precinct; Letter; Page; Year; Names; Signature of Applicant; Residence, May 1, 188-; Age; Place of Birth; Occupation; Place of Business; Date of Naturalization, Name and Location of Court; Residence at Date of Naturalization.

Alfred J. Ashton, 256 No Harvard, 22, Stantonbury, Eng., clerk, Allston, US Cir. Ct. Boston, Sep 25, 1889, same

Michael Burke, Market, 26, Co. Galway, Ireland, wool sorter, No. Beacon St., US Dist. Ct Boston, Oct 15, 1886, No. Beacon

Matthew Oman, 458 Western Ave., 33, Finland, Russia, Carpenter, Car Shops Allston, US. Dist. Ct. Oct 13, 1888, same

Anthony J. Rossi, 321 Market St., 52, Marcott, Canton of Gessin, Switzerland, Clergyman, Brighton, Sup. Ct. Suffolk Co., May 24, 1871, same

Daniel Sullivan, 9 Lincoln St., 35, Co. Cork, Ireland, Laborer, Brighton, Herkimer Co. NY, County Court, Oct 27, 1887, same

Ward 10; Precinct 5, Register 1-4; 1896–1897 [organized by street]

Headings: Date of Application; Line[unknown reference]; Page[unknown reference]; Number of Residences or other Designation May 1st, 1896; Name; Signature; Term of Residence: State, City, Ward; Occupation; Place of Occupation; Place of Birth; Court; Date of Papers; Personal Description: Age, Height, Weight; Present Residence.

Sep 28, 1897; N; 140; 2nd fl, 291; Frank M. Lynch; Frank M. Lynch; -; 7; Salesman; 33 Summer St.; Springfield, Ms; - ; - ; 29; 5/8; 122; 148 Chandler St.

Sep 25, 1897; H; 107; suite 4, 9; James McHugh; James McHugh; -; 9 ;-; Lab.; - ; Donegal, Ireland; U.S. Cirt. Boston; Nov 7, '94; 27; 5/9; 194; 3 Dartmouth pl.

Jun 24, 1896; T; 136; 4th fl., 131; Walter J. Rhodes; Walter J. Rhodes; 8y; 5y ;2y; Clerk; 172 Columbus Ave.; England; Police Ct. Haverhill; Walter J. son of James Thomas, Jul 7, 1892; 24; 5/4 1/2; 115; Dartmouth St.

Nov 27, 1897; F; 169; 3rd fl, 12; William M. Rowan; William M. Rowan;-; 3 ;- ; Barber; Hotel Vendome; Canada; Fathers papers (William Rowan) Sup. Ct., New Haven Conn; Oct 21, 1884; 38; 5/4;160; 16 Truro St. [over age when Father nat., appeared here later & admitted over age when Father nat.]

Sep 3, 1896; p ;158; 33; John Ellis; John Ellis; 20; 20; 2; Salesman; 33 Summer St.; Co. Clare, Ireland; US Circt. Ct., Boston; Aug 30, 1878; 52; 5/7; 187; Thetford Ave., Dorchester

Oct 11, 1897; E; 146; 133; Edward O. McBean; Edward O. McBean; 20; 20; 1; Porter; Bristol Hotel; Island St. Croix, W.I.; US Dist. Ct. Boston, Mass; Oct 11, 1883; 46; 5/7; 160; Dartmouth St.

Voter lists including naturalization dates and venues are exciting to researchers of immigrants who lived in Boston. The lists of women voters are even more exciting. Women could vote in Boston school elections beginning in 1888, and those of foreign birth were also required to explain why they were entitled to vote. This could mean that they married a native-born man, or if their husbands were foreign-born, they could give the date and court of naturalization, or it may be the date and court of naturalization of their father-in-laws

SOME EXAMPLES

Ward 19, 1888–1903:

1894, Marie E. Coleman, 15 Warwick St., 35, Montreal Can., housewife, husband (Hiram H.) born in Lynchburg, WV.

1901, Nellie J. Dillon, 28 Mindoro St., 22, Boston MA, Filler, Roxbury Carpet Co.

1895, Dorothea C. Hayes, Hotel Westminster, 25, Hanover Germany, housewife, husband (Otis H.) native born

1894, Minnie O. Scott, 69 Cabot St., 26, Greensboro NC, housewife

Catherine Slowe, 9 Liberty St., 40, Ireland, housekeeper, U.S. Dist. Ct., Boston, Oct 15, 1898, husband's paper Michael

1892–1899:

1897, Harriet E. Lothrop, 571 Columbus Ave., 39, b. Taunton, Physician, 571 Columbus Ave.

1899, Luella K. Leavitt, 28 St. James Ave., 33, Concord NH, Librarian, Boston Pub. Lib.

1899, Margaret J. Magennis, 44 Union Park, 65, Ireland, Journalist - Traveller

1892, Adelaide Pray, 37 Austin St., 28, P.E. Island, husband James H. born in Gardiner ME

1906 to 1918:

1908, Henrietta S. Fines, 9 Allen St., 27, Vienna Austria, housekeeper, husband Fathers Papers (Simeon) US Cir. Ct. Boston Dec 4, 1897

1911, Susan B. Jameson, 17 Dix St., 26, Warren OH, Stenographer, 10 Tremont St., single

1914, Ella Wallace, 307 Cambridge St., 35, Evanston IL, housewife, husband John L. born in Marshalltown, IA

1915, Elizabeth C. ODwyer, 16 Rockland Ave., 42, Co. Kerry, Ireland, housewife, husband (Myles) born Co. Cork, Ireland, Police Ct. Brockton, Oct 16, 1900

City of Boston, Register of Women Voters, 1920

Headings: Date, Ward, Precinct, name, signature, residence April 1, age, place of birth, occupation and place of business, court and date of naturalization, if married woman husband's name and birthplace, present residence.

Ruth M. Tisdale, 126 Newbury St., 27, Boston, MA, secretary 10 Tremont st., Boston

Bernice E. Metcalf, 27 Cotton St., 34, Baldwinsmill, Quebec, Canada, housewife, wife of Arthur Metcalf, born in Boston, MA

Elizabeth Musculus, 72 Ardale St., 51, Ahmis, Germany, housewife, wife of Wm. F. born in Bessen, Ger., US Dist. Ct., Boston, Nov 19, 1894.

Theresa M.J. Kien, 376 Grove St., 41, Alsace Loraine, France, housewife, Wife of August His Father paper William Prussia, Germany, US Cir Ct Boston, Mass Jul 5, 1888

Virginia W. Matthews, 105 Clement Ave., 44, Boothbay Harbor, ME, Housewife, wife of Russell V. born in Brighton, MA

Katherine Thompson, 337 Cornell St., 42, Co. Cavan, Ireland, housewife, wife of Andrew J. born in Liverpool Eng., US Cir Ct. Boston Nov 12, 1918

Edith S. Watson, 274 Belgrade Rd., 39 Bradford, England, housewife, wife of Joseph born in Halifax Eng. US Dist. Ct. Prov. RI, Sep 19, 1903

15 TEACHERS' RECORDS

The BCA has the records of teachers in the Boston schools from 1876 to 1952, though records less than seventy years old are closed for privacy reasons. Most of the records are short, such as "Lucy M.A. Redding – 5th grade – resigned from Eliot September 1, 1879," or "Alice M. Jordan (Mrs. Porter) – In Horace Mann School for the Deaf – Resigned November 1, 1880 – married – Certificate renewed June 16, 1902." In many cases, though, more detail is included:

Julius Eichberg, Special grade master
    Director of Music in Boston Schools 1880
    "Special Instructor of Music" high schools from April 1, 1884
    Resigned April 1, 1887.

Sarah E. Gould – 5th grade – Sherwin District – 4th Assistant
    Elected to serve during the pleasure of the School Committee April 1, 1889
    Retired on pension to take effect August 31, 1921
    Died September 16, 1939

Mrs. Sarah C. Woodward
    Special Grade February 1,1888, Instructor in the Schools of Cookery; 4th grade qualification
    In 1887 age 32. Graduate of high school, New Haven, Conn. Has taught six years in the intermediate and grammar grades; four and a half years in New Haven, Conn., and 1 year and a half in Pueblo, Colorado.
    Appointed instructor in the schools of cookery, February 1, 1888 on probation. Confirmed February 12, 1889. Resigned January 1, 1890.

Lucy G.M. Card – graduated 1877
    34 Regent St., Roxbury
    Substituted in Sherman Dist., 2 days, 1878
    Appointed special asst. Dudley Dist. April 25, 1883
        Temp. Third Asst. Dudley September 3 to 14 1883
        Temp. Third Asst. Dudley February 4, 1884

Reappointed May 5, 1884

Appointed Special Asst. Comins Dist. April 23, 1885

Appointed Temp. Third Asst. Dudley October 5 to 30 1885

During 1885 and 1886 substituted in grammar and primary schools

Appointed Temp. 4th Asst. Dudley October 10, 1887

Again on January 3, 1888

Elected to serve during the pleasure of the school committee June 1892

Retired on pension to take effect December 31, 1923

Died January 13, 1929

16 PASSENGER LISTS

B oston has been very important as a port city, from the first arrival of the Winthrop fleet in 1630 to the present day. While a few passenger lists exist, and research has been done to identify the probable ship on which many immigrants arrived, most surviving passenger lists date from 1848.

NARA has indexes to Boston passengers lists from 1848 to 1891, 1902 to 1906, and 1906 to 1920, as well as from 1820 to 1943. BPL also has the index from 1848 to 1891, the lists from 1820 to 1891, and 1901 to 1920. ARCH has the index and lists from 1848 to 1891.

On the NEHGS website is a database for alien passengers to the Port of Boston, 1847 to 1852. This database draws from lists prepared by the Superintendent of the Port of Boston, for the use of the overseers of the poor in the Commonwealth of Massachusetts. The information from January 1, 1847, to January 1, 1851 was compiled from various sources, but after the 1851 the list was issued monthly. The records give the name of the passenger, date of arrival, ship's name, passenger's age, and place of birth. In the later years comments about the condition of the passenger upon arrival may also have been included. For example, John Sullivan arrived 2 June 1851 on the *Jane Glasson* from Liverpool. He was age fifty, his last residence was Ireland, he was a servant, and was "Old and used up."

Early passenger lists do not contain much information. For the passengers of the ship *George Marshall*, which arrived on March 28, 1857, the list gives the name, age, sex, occupation, and the country to which each passenger belonged. By the end of the century, the lists provide considerably more information. For example, the *Pavonia* arrived at Boston in 1897. There was one passenger on board named Alice Gillespie for whom the following information was given: age 18; single; a servant; able to read and write; of Irish nationality; last residence was Donegal; final destination is Philadelphia though she did not have a ticket to get there; she paid her own passage; had

$5.30; had not been in the U.S. before; was going to her uncle Pat Brennan in Philadelphia; she had never been supported by charity; was not a polygamist; was not under constraint to labor in the U.S.; her health was good; and she was not deformed or crippled.

17 Naturalization Records

The NARA has photographic negatives (dexigraphs) of naturalization records from all federal and non-federal Massachusetts courts from 1790 to 1906. They also have naturalization records from the U.S. district and circuit courts through 1971.

In the 1930s, one of the projects of the Work Projects Administration (WPA) was to index naturalizations in the federal, state, county, and municipal courts in New England (except Connecticut) from 1790 to 1906. This index is on microfilm at the NARA, NEHGS, BPL, and FHL. The cards in this index are organized using the soundex system, the same system used to index the 1880, 1900, and 1920 Federal censuses. This method groups surnames that "sound alike" and eliminates some of the searching to make sure all or most variations of the surname have been checked. Until 1920, there was very little reason for women to become citizens, since they became citizens if their husbands were citizens or naturalized, so this index is primarily of men.

The cards should list the person's name, address, certificate number or volume and page, title and location of court, country of birth or allegiance, date of birth or age, date and port of arrival in U.S., and date of naturalization. With the name of the court, and the volume and page, you can then ask to see the dexigraph of the naturalization record at NARA.

In New England, the dexigraph is the most likely document to give you an exact date of birth and/or place of birth. Beginning with the information on naturalization from the Boston men's and women's voter lists, I found the following:

> In the voters list Isaac G. Newcomb, age fifty-one and born in Cornwallis, Nova Scotia, says he was naturalized in the U.S. District Court in Boston on September 17, 1892. The naturalization records show that on September 17, 1892, Isaac G. Newcomb was indeed naturalized in the U.S. district court. He was born in Cornwallis, Nova Scotia, April 25, 1851, and arrived at the port of Boston on April 12, 1866. His witnesses were Clarence E. Learned and Geo. W. Martin.

Walter J. Rhodes applied as a voter on June 24, 1896 at age twenty-four. He says he is a citizen because his father, James Thomas Rhodes was naturalized in the Haverhill Police Court on July 7, 1892. On July 11, 1892, James Thomas Rhodes was naturalized in the Haverhill Police Court. He was born in London, County Middlesex, England, February 16, 1842. He arrived at the port of New York on June 20, 1887. His witnesses were Arthur W. Johnson and Fred R. Downes.

John Ellis applied as a voter on September 3, 1896 at age fifty-two and was born in Co. Clare, Ireland. He says he naturalized in the U.S. circuit court in Boston on August 30, 1878. On August 30, 1878 John Ellis of Boston was naturalized in the U.S. Circuit Court. He was born in Co. Clare, Ireland, December 1, 1854. He arrived at the port of New York on February 7, 1861. His witnesses were Andrew McCormick and John Young.

In the 1888–1904 Register of Women Voters, Catherine Slowe, age forty, born Ireland, says she is a citizen by right of her husband Michael Slowe who naturalized in the U.S. District Court in Boston October 15, 1898. On October 15, 1898, Michael Slowe of Boston naturalized in the U.S. District Court. He was born in Co. Galway, Ireland, on September 25, 1864 and arrived at the port of Philadelphia on May 2, 1889. His witnesses were James Lally and Martin Lally.

In the 1920 Register of Women Voters, Theresa M.J. Kein, born Alsace Lorraine, France, says she is a voter by right of her husband, August Kien's father, William Kien, who was naturalized at the U.S. Circuit Court on July 5, 1888. On July 5, 1888 William Kein of Norwood was naturalized in the U.S. Circuit Court. He was born in Germany on October 12, 1843 and arrived at the port of New York on November 25, 1881. His witnesses were Jacob Bayer and John W. Foster.

Be sure to take note of the witnesses' names, as they may be family or friends from "the old country" who immigrated earlier. Several years ago, I researched a group of glass workers who came from England to Boston in the early 1800s. On most of their naturalizations one of the witnesses was the owner of the glass works in Boston and the other was a worker who had come earlier and was already naturalized.

If you are looking for a female immigrant, you may be able to determine her place of birth by finding the naturalization record of a father, brother, uncle, or cousin. Names of these male relatives, if they were Catholic, may come from the sponsors of children's baptisms or the witnesses of a marriage. You may also find connected people living in the same household in a census or, if you are dealing with an unusual surname, by just searching all the vital records of others of that surname.

18 Immigrants in Print

For general information on immigrants to Boston, consult:

Price, Michael and Anthony Mitchell Sammarco, *Boston's Immigrants 1840–1925* (Charleston, SC, 2000).

IRISH IMMIGRANTS

The Search for Missing Friends, Irish Immigrant Advertisements Placed in the Boston Pilot (NEHGS); also available on CD from NEHGS.

Vol. 1, 1831–1850, Ruth-Ann M. Harris & Donald M. Jacobs (1989)

Vol. 2, 1851–1853, Ruth-Ann M. Harris & B. Emer O'Keefe (1991)

Vol. 3, 1854–1856, Ruth-Ann M. Harris & B. Emer O'Keefe (1993)

Vol. 4, 1857–1860, Ruth-Ann M. Harris & B. Emer O'Keefe (1995)

Vol. 5, 1861–1865, B. Emer O'Keefe (1996)

Vol. 6, 1866–1870, B. Emer O'Keefe (1997)

Vol. 7, 1871–1876, B. Emer O'Keefe (1999)

Vol. 8, 1877–1920, B. Emer O'Keefe (1999)

As the introduction to this series states:

> The destruction of the potato crop four years in succession caused Ireland's population to decline from 8.2 million in 1841 to 6.5 million in 1851. While Ireland was emptying, Boston was filling with Irish immigrants, showing a ten-year increase of 105 percent. From 1846 to 1849, 100,000 Irish persons arrived in Boston. Most immigrants would expect to obtain their first employment through family networks of siblings, uncles, nephews and sons who had preceded them to America. Ireland was a society in which obligations and claims among kin were extremely powerful and disregarded only at the cost of severing family ties permanently. However, many immigrants would discover after

arrival that it was not enough to know only the name of the town where they had last heard from their relative. America was a much larger country than the new arrivals could ever have imagined, and following the employment trail could easily take them hundreds of miles from where they had begun.

Therefore, many Irish turned to the *Boston Pilot* and placed advertisements to try and locate their missing relatives and friends. Almost all these entries identify specific places in Ireland where they came from. While the persons inquiring and those being looked for can be from all over the country, many are from Boston or passed through Boston, as these examples show:

Of EDWARD TIERNEY, native of Newtown, parish of Burriscarra, co. Mayo, who landed in Boston in the Spring of 1848. He left Boston in May, 1849, for Vermont in company with Martin Foy and Patrick Coulter, and not heard from since. Any information respecting him will be thankfully received by his brother, THOMAS TIERNEY, Hopkinton, Massachusetts.

Of PATRICK KELLY, a native of Dublin, who came to this country in June, 1849 - landed in Boston - when last heard from was at No. 63 Atkinson street, Boston. Any information respecting him will be thankfully received by JOHN QUIN, care of S.S. Thompson, Lancaster, N.H.

TIMOTHY B. MURPHY and son, JOHN ENGLAND MURPHY, left Pittsburgh 11th April, 1846. He was a mathematical teacher. When last heard of was in Glenburine, 5 miles from Kingston, Upper Canada, teaching school. The Boy is going on 15 years old. Any information respecting them will be thankfully received by his wife & younger son. Direct to MARGARET H. MURPHY, No. 15 Belmont street, Boston, Ms.

Of JOHN CLEARY, and his brothers, THOMAS, MICHAEL or WILLIAM CLEARY, natives of Ballyphilip, co. Tipperary - emigrated to this country in 1849 - supposed to be in Boston. Any information respecting them will be thankfully received by their brother, PATRICK CLEARY, Conshocken, Montgomery County, Pa.

Ryan, Dennis P. *A Journey Through Boston Irish History* (Charleston, 1999).

Cullen, James Bernard, *The Story of the Irish in Boston* (Boston, 1889; photoduplication NEHGS).

JEWISH IMMIGRANTS

Blatt, Warren, *Resources for Jewish Genealogy in the Boston Area* (Boston, 1996).

Smith, Ellen and Jonathan D. Sarna, *The Jews of Boston* (Boston, 1995).

GREEK IMMIGRANTS

Voultsos, Mary, *Greek Immigrant Passengers, Port of Boston, 1902–1906* (Worcester, c1993).
  This index includes the passenger's name and age, the vessel, and the date the ship arrived at the port of Boston.

ITALIAN IMMIGRANTS

Colletta, John Philip, *Finding Italian Roots*, 2nd edition (Baltimore, 2003).

DeMarco, William M., *Ethnics and Enclaves: Boston's Italian North End* (Ann Arbor, MI, c1981).
  This is a reprint of a revision of a Ph. D. thesis.

FRENCH IMMIGRANTS

Forbes, Allan, *The Boston French* (State Street Bank, Boston, 1889).

SWEDISH IMMIGRANTS

Wretlind, Eric, *A Swedish City Directory of Boston, 1881* (Winter Park, FL, c1986).

19 SOME MISCELLANEOUS SOURCES

The Boston Police Department, Records Center and Archives collections include photographs, the Brink's Robbery investigation files, diaries of police officers, Police Department Annual Reports, rare books, scrapbooks, and more.

There are several good photographic collections in Boston repositories. These include the Bostonian Society, BPL, Historic New England, and MSA. The illustrations in this book are from the Bostonian Society collection.

Permits for Demolished Buildings, 1871 to present, and photographs of school buildings, ca. 1900–1970, and condemned buildings, 1951 to 1990, are available at BCA.

The Ancient and Honorable Artillery Company of Massachusetts is the oldest chartered military organization in the western hemisphere. Its charter was granted in March 1638 by Governor John Winthrop. It was chartered as an Independent Company to train officers for the existing militias. There is a four-volume history, and in 1895 they published a Roll of Members through 1894. They have a small library, primarily of military books, and are currently working on organizing the records of later members. The history of The Ancient and Honorable Artillery Company has short biographies of members under the year in which they joined. A typical example is Joseph Ford who joined in 1786:

> Joseph Ford was a shop-keeper in Boston, at No. 65 Cornhill, in 1789, but in 1796 had retired, and lived on Eliot Street. He was a son of "Joseph and Perslla [Priscilla] Ford," and was born in Braintree, Sept. 18, 1740. Aug. 14, 1772, he had, in Boston, a wife named Hannah. He was active in the militia, and rose to the grade of captain.

> Capt. Ford died suddenly, in Boston, Nov. 17, 1797, aged fifty-six years.

> The Columbian Centinel said of him: "He was an irreproachable professor of

the Christian religion, a sincere friend to his country, and a uniform example of conscientious, kind, and inoffensive behavior, in all the relations of domestic and public life."

The Grand Lodge of Massachusetts [Masons] has information on members, though for early members it may be quite limited. Their Samuel Crocker Lawrence Library and Museum in Boston houses the finest Masonic Library in North America. Many of the members of the Ancient and Honorable Artillery Company were also Masons.

20 BOSTON IN PRINT

For many of these titles, I have included short explanations or quotations from the introductions to give some idea of the material covered. This list may not include all the books mentioned in the text of this book.

The State Street Bank and Trust Company has published several small books and booklets:

Boston England and Boston New England 1630–1930 (1930).

Boston-One Hundred Years a City. A Collection of Views Made from Rare Prints and Old Photographs Showing the Changes Which Have Occurred in Boston During One Hundred Years of its Existence as a City, 1822–1922 (1922).

Forty of Boston's Historic Houses. A Brief Illustrated Description of the Residences of Historic Characters of Boston who have Lived in or Near the Business Section (1912).

Boston's Growth. A Bird's Eye View of Boston's Increase in Territory and Population From It's Beginning to the Present (1910).

Mayors of Boston – An Illustrated Epitome of Who the Mayors Have Been and What They Have Done (1914).

Some Events of Boston and Its Neighbors (1917).

Some Interesting Boston Events (1916).

Boston and Some Noted Emigres: A Collection of Facts and Incidents with Appropriate Illustrations Relating to Some Well-Known Citizens of France who Found Homes in Boston and New England... (1938).

Some Statues of Boston: Some Reproductions of Some of the Statues for which Boston is Famous, with Information Concerning the Personalities and Events so Memorialized (1946).

Other Statues of Boston: Reproductions of Other Statues of Boston as a Sequel to Our Brochure of 1946 (1947).

Boston's Story in Inscriptions: Being Reproductions of the Markings That are or Have Been on Historic Sites (1908)

Forty of Boston's Immortals: Showing Illustrations and Giving a Brief Sketch of Forty Men of the Past Whose Work Entitle Them to a Niche in a Boston Hall of Fame (1910).

Yankee Ship Sailing Cards: Presenting Reproductions of Some of the Colorful Cards Announcing Ship Sailings in the Days When Boston Ships and Boston Men Were Known in Every Port of the Seven Seas (1948).

Pilots and Pilot Boats of Boston Harbor: Presenting Stories and Illustrations of the Skilled, Resourceful Men of Stout Hearts Who, with Their Trim, Weatherly Boats of Sturdy Construction, have Played such an Important Role in the Maritime Life of Boston (1956).

Old Shipping Days in Boston (1918).

Old Shipping Days in Boston (1969).

Some Merchants and Sea Captains of Old Boston: Being a Collection of Sketches of Notable Men and Mercantile Houses Prominent During the Early Half of the Nineteenth Century in the Commerce and Shipping of Boston (1918).

Other Merchants and Sea Captains of Old Boston: Being More Information About the Merchants and Sea Captains of Old Boston Who Played Such an Important Part in Building up the Commerce of New England Together with Some Quaint and Curious Stories of the Sea (1919).

Some Ships of the Clipper Ship Era: Their Builders, Owners, and Captains. A Glance at an Interesting Phase of the American Merchant Marine so far as it Relates to Boston (1913).

State Street: A Brief Account of a Boston Way (1906).

State Street Events: A Brief Account of Diverse Notable Persons and Sundry Stirring Events Having to do with the History of this Ancient Street (1916).

The Log of the State Street Trust Company: Containing a Description of its Colonial Banking Rooms, its Ship Models, Quaint Furnishings, Rare Prints of Ships and Views of Boston and Other New England Towns-Including a Story of the 'Lamp Shade Fleet' and Sketches of the Company's Staff, with a Story of the National Union Bank and a Chapter on the Significance of State Street as a Business Centre (1926).

Leaves from the Log of the State Street Trust Company: Containing a Brief Description of its Colonial Banking Rooms, its Ship Models, Quaint Furnishings, Rare Prints of Ships, Views of Boston and Other New England Towns – Including the 'Lamp Shade Fleet,' Trust Department Rooms and the Aviation Collection at our Union Trust Office. Also a note on the Significance of State Street as a Business Centre (1949).

The Second National Bank of Boston (1975).

Copley Square: A Brief Description of Its History Including a Short Sketch of the Famous Artist for Whom the Square was Named-With Illustrations of Interesting Buildings, Protraits by Copley and Early Views (1941).

Baltzell, E. Digby, *Puritan Boston and Quaker Philadelphia, Two Protestant Ethics and the Spirit of Class, Authority and Leadership* (New York, 1979).

Blatt, Warren, *Resources for Jewish Genealogy in the Boston Area* (Boston, 1996). An excellent guide to researching Jewish ancestors in Boston, but much of this book would also be useful to those who descend from anyone who immigrated to Boston in late nineteenth and early twentieth centuries. Especially useful are the sections on naturalizations and passenger lists.

Casaburi, Victor F., A *Colonial History of East Boston* (East Boston, 1975).

Chamberlain, Allen, *Beacon Hill: Its Ancient Pastures and Early Mansions* (Boston, 1925).

Davis, Charlotte Pease, *Directory of Massachusetts Place Names (Massachusetts DAR, 1987).* Did you know that at one time, the following were names sections of Boston? Aberdeen, Academy Hill, Barry's Corner, Belle Isle, Boylston, Canterbury, Clarendon Hills, Fairmount, Germantown, Hazelwood, Hommfield, Jeffries Point, Nonantum Hill, Parker Hill, Rocky Hill, Rugby, Spectakle Island, Sunnyside, Washington Village, and Wellington Hill.

Drake, Samuel Gardner, *The History and Antiquities of Boston...from its Settlement in 1630, to the Year 1770* (Boston, 1856).

Formisano, Ronald P. & Constance K. Burns, *BOSTON 1700–1980, The Evolution of Urban Politics* (Westport, CT, 1980). This book is "a series of essays dealing with each major phase of Boston's politics, from the eighteenth-century town meeting which became so visible in the American Revolution to the contemporary city managed by a four-term mayor (1969–83) and a large, if fragmented, bureaucracy. Although the essays differ in their approaches, methods, and foci, this anthology provides in broad outline a virtually continuous narrative of the structure and dynamics of Boston's politics at each distinctive phase of its development from the 1700s to the 1970s."

Gardner-Wescott, *Massachusetts Sources, Part I: Boston, New Bedford, Springfield, Worcester* (Boston, Massachusetts Society of Genealogists, 1988). A listing of libraries, archives, and institutions and their holdings, which may be of use to researchers. Since it was published twelve years ago, some of the information is now out of date, but overall it is still very useful.

Haskell, John D., Massachusetts: *A Bibliography of Its History* (Boston, 1976).

Historical Data Relating to Counties, Cities and Towns in Massachusetts (Boston, 1997).

> This is the easiest guide for finding when towns were absorbed into Boston: Roxbury, 1867; Dorchester, 1869; Charlestown, 1873; Brighton, 1873; West Roxbury, 1873; and Hyde Park, 1912. In 1870 and 1874, parts of Brookline were annexed and in 1875 a part of Boston was annexed to Newton. These dates are very important when looking for probate and land records of your ancestors, since most of these towns, when separate from Boston, were not in Suffolk County; before annexation, therefore you must search another county and after annexation, you search Suffolk County.

Holbrook, Jay Mack, *Boston Beginnings 1630–1699* (Oxford, MA, 1980).

> An alphabetical list of people who were in Boston in the seventeenth century compiled from a variety of sources, including members of First Church, Second Church, First Baptist Church, Old South Church, those who took the oath of allegiance, tax lists, and land owners.

Horton, James Oliver & Lois E. Horton, *Black Bostonians, Family Life and Community Struggle in the Antebellum North* (New York, 1979).

> "Unlike most histories, this book studies those individuals who were neither rich nor politically powerful. In this sense, it is a social history of working people. It is unique among studies of black history in that it examines the lives of pre-Civil War blacks, most of whom were not slaves themselves and did not live in the region of slavery. This is not a book of 'first blacks.' Individual achievement is seen as most important within the context of family, group, or community membership. This study moves beyond previous works to place discrimination and social protest in the context of family and community life."

Kirker, Harold, *Bulfinch's Boston, 1787–1817* (New York, 1964).

Knights, Peter R., *Yankee Destinies, The Lives of Ordinary Nineteenth-Century Bostonians* (Chapel Hill, 1991).

Knights, Peter R., *The Plain People of Boston, 1830–1860: A Study in City Growth* (New York, 1971).

Krieger, Alex and David Cobb, *Mapping Boston* (Cambridge, 1999).

> *New England Ancestors* (Spring 2001, 2:17) says "The book includes both historical maps of the city and maps that show the gradual emergence of the New England region from the imaginations of explorers to a form that we would recognize today. Each map is accompanied by a full description and by a short essay offering an insight into its context. The essays, by Anne Mackin, discuss people both familiar and unknown, landmarks, and signigicant events in shaping the landscape and life of the city. Highlights of the

book are a series of new maps detailing Boston's growth, a timeline and chronology of significant dates in Boston's development, and a glossary of cartographic terms."

Levesque, George A., *Black Boston: African American Life and Culture in Urban America, 1750–1860* (New York, 1994).

List of Maps of Boston, Published Between 1614 and 1822, Reprint of Appendix J, Annual Report of the City Engineer (Boston, 1902).
Descriptions of maps including date, size, area covered, scale, and other details, such as maps showing fortifications and gun batteries during the Revolution; and places such as where these maps can be found, such as the Massachusetts Historical Society, the Bostonian Society, and the Harvard College Library. At the end is a list of printed maps of Boston.

Loring, James Spear, *The Hundred Boston Orators Appointed By the Municipal Authorities and Other Public Bodies, From 1770 to 1852; Comprising Historical Gleanings, Illustrating the Principles and Progress of Our Republican Institutions* (Boston, 1853).

Melnyk, Marcia D., *Genealogist's Handbook for New England Research* (Boston, 1999).
This is primarily a "where to" book for researchers. It contains information on each of the New England states and the repositories where one can do research, including directions to find the repository.

Noyes, Sybil, Charles Thornton Libby, and Walter Goodwin Davis, *Genealogical Dictionary of Maine and New Hampshire* (reprint, Baltimore, 1976).
During the Indian Wars, many families moved from Maine to Boston, so check this book for any clues.

O'Connor, Thomas H., *Fitzpatrick's Boston, 1846–1866: John Bernard Fitzpatrick, Third Bishop of Boston* (Boston, 1984).

O'Connor, Thomas H., *South Boston: My Home Town, The History of an Ethnic Neighborhood* (Boston, 1988, reprint, 1994)

Publications of The Colonial Society of Massachusetts

Volume 9, "Check-List of Boston Newspapers 1704–1780"

Volume 29 & 30, "Records of the Suffolk County Court 1671–1680"

Volume 46, "Boston Prints and Printmakers 1670–1773"

Volume 48, "Boston Furniture of the Eighteenth Century"
[An upcoming volume of Almshouse Records will contain much information on the residents of the almshouse, including many deaths. The introduction will give a great amount of information on life in Boston.]

Price, Michael and Anthony Mitchell Sammarco, *Boston's Immigrants 1840–1925* (Charleston, S.C., 2000).

Rutman, Darrett B., *Winthrop's Boston, Portrait of A Puritan Town, 1630–1649* (Williamsburg, VA, 1865).

Schweitzer, George K., *Massachusetts Genealogical Research* (Knoxville, TN, 1990).
    A good, basic book on doing genealogical research in Massachusetts. Since this book is ten years old, some aspects of it are out of date, such as the descriptions of where in a particular library or archive a source is located. NEHGS, especially, has undergone extensive renovations since this book was published. But the described sources will still be there!

Simonds, Thomas C., *History of South Boston: formerly Dorchester Neck; Now Ward XII of the City of Boston* (Boston, 1857).

Sumner, William H., *A History of East Boston, with Biographical Sketches of its Early Proprietors* (Boston, 1858).

Thwing, Annie Haven, *The Crooked and Narrow Streets of Boston* (Boston, 1925).

Toomey, John J. & Edward P.B. Rankin, *History of South Boston (Its Past and Present)* (Boston, 1901).

Trinkaus-Randall, Gregor, *Massachusetts Special Collections Directory* (Boston, 1999).
    Contains information on the special collections in 39 libraries, archives, and reposititories in Boston. Gives contact information, hours, holdings, collection description, access, copying, and finding guides.

Winsor, Justin, *The Memorial History of Boston, Including Suffolk County, Massachusetts, 1630–1880*, 4 volumes (Boston, 1880-1881).

21 TOWNS THAT ARE NOW PART OF BOSTON

Charlestown Land Records, 1638–1802, Boston Record Commissioners Report, Vol. 3, 2nd. Ed., (Boston, 1883).

Hunnewell, James F., *Records of the First Church in Charlestown, Massachusetts, 1632–1789* (Boston, 1880).

Hunnewell, James F., *A Century of Town Life: A History of Charlestown, Massachusetts, 1775–1887* (Boston, 1888).

Joslyn, Roger D., *Vital Records of Charlestown, Massachusetts, To the Year 1850*, 2 Vols. (Boston, 1984, 1995).

Wyman, Thomas Bellows, *The Genealogies and Estates of Charlestown, In the County of Middlesex and Commonwealth of Massachusetts, 1629–1818*, 2 Vols. (Boston, 1879).

Chamberlain, Mellen, *A Documentary History of Chelsea, Including the Boston Precincts of Winnisimmet, Rumney Marsh and Pullen Point, 1624–1824*, 2 Vols. (Boston, 1908).

Dorchester Town Records, 1632–1691, Boston Record Commissioners Report, Vol. 4, 2nd. Ed., (Boston, 1883).

Vital Records of the Town of Dorchester to 1825, Boston Record Commissioners Report, Vol. 21 (Boston, 1891).

Vital Records of the Town of Dorchester from 1826-1849, Boston Record Commissioners Report, Vol. 36 (Boston, 1905).

Tax Payers, Town of Dorchester, 1849–1869, (Boston, 1849–1869).

Records of the First Church at Dorchester in New England, 1636–1734 (Boston, 1891).

History of the Town of Dorchester, Massachusetts (Boston, 1859).

Shurtleff, Benjamin, *The History of the Town of Revere* (Boston, 1938).

Roxbury Land Records and Church Records, Boston Record Commissioners Report, VI, 2nd Ed., (Boston, 1884).

The Town of Roxbury, Its Memorable Persons and Places, Boston Record Commissioners Report, Vol. 34 (Boston, 1905).

Robert J. Dunkle and Ann S. Lainhart, *The Town Records of Roxbury, Massachusetts, 1647 to 1730* (Boston, 1997). [Volume 2 is on microfilm at NEHGS]

Ellis, Charles Mayo, *The History of Roxbury Town* (Dedham, 1848).

Clark, William H., *The History of Winthrop, Massachusetts, 1630–1952* (Winthrop, 1952).

22 ARTICLES ON BOSTON FAMILIES

If you are researching a family that lived in Boston, I recommend reading some of the following articles from *The New England Historical and Genealogical Register, The American Genealogist,* and *The Mayflower Descendant.* This list is not comprehensive. They will give you ideas on how to use many of the records I have mentioned in this book. Seeing how someone else approached a problem may help you solve a problem. These are in alphabetical order of the surname.

Many of these articles run over more than one issue or more than one volume. I have given only the first volume and page of the article.

Lesure, Frank G., "The Children of John[3] **Adams** (1661–1702) of Braintree and Boston, Maltster," *TAG* 71:21.

Wead, Frederick W., "Nathaniel **Adams** of Weymouth and Boston, Mass.," *TAG,* 30:65.

Lainhart, Ann S. and Alicia Crane Williams, "Hepzibah **Alden**'s Silver Box, The Scandal of Ann Sargent Gage and Some Descendants of Nathaniel[3] (John[2-1]) Alden," *MD* 45:1.

Lainhart, Ann S., "The Probable Wife of John[3] (John[2-1]) **Alden**," *MD* 47:1.

Lainhart, Ann S., "Mixed Up Marys and Elizabeths in the Family of John[2] **Alden**," *MD* 47:101.

Armstrong see **Talby**

Cook, Wendell B., "William **Badlam**, Ship Master of Boston and Weymouth and Some of His Descendants," *NEHGR,* 140:3.

Barclay, Mrs. John E. and Rachel E., "**Barlow, Coombs**, and **Warren** of Boston," *TAG* 46:129.

Fradd, Brandon, "A New Royal Descent for Christopher[1] **Batt**," *TAG* 79:85.

Holman, Winifred Lovering, "**Beadon-Bedon** Family," *TAG* 35:171.

Harris, Gale Ion, "Thomas[1] **Bell**, Boston Executioner, and His Son Thomas[2] Bell of Stonington, Connecticut," *TAG* 74:281.

Noyes, Charles P., "George **Bethune** of Craigfurdies, Scotland, and Boston, Mass.," *NEHGR* 60:238.

Barclay, Mrs. John E., "Abigail Arnold, Wife of Solomon[3] **Blake** of Dorchester, Mass." [Bateman], *TAG* 35:207.

Hartman, J. Crawford, "John **Blanchard** of Boston, Mass. And Some of His Descendants," *NEHGR* 93:162.

Pitman, H. Minot, "Descendants of John **Blower** of Boston," *TAG* 21:237.

Montgomery, Robert H., "Zacheus **Bosworth**, of Boston, Husbandman," *TAG* 24:80.

Fiske, Jane Fletcher, "Some Additions to Torrey's Marriages: Trerise, Lynde, **Bourne**," *NEHGR* 159:235.

Harris, Gale Ion, "Peter **Brackett** of Braintree and Boston, With Notes on His Daughter, Sarah (Brackett) (Shaw) (Benjamin) Jimmerson," *NEHGR* 155:279.

Lainhart, Ann S., and Scott Andrew Bartley, "*Non-Mayflower* **Bradfords** of New England: Descendants of Robert Bradford of Boston," *MD* 53:1.

Coddington, John Insley, "The Family of Henry **Bridgman** of Thelnetham, Co. Suffolk, England, and Boston, Mass.," *TAG* 33:113.

Harris, Gale Ion, "William[1] and Mary **Brigg**s of Boston and the Connecticut Valley with Notes on their Sons-in-Law John Harris and Wolston Brockway," *NEHGR* 151:87.

Barclay, Mrs. John E., "The **Brough** Family of Marshfield and Boston," *TAG* 37:212.

Chamberlain, George Walter, "Old Boston Families: The **Bryant** Family," *NEHGR* 96:321.

Montgomery, Robert H., "James **Butler,** Vintner, of Boston: A Critique of 'Butleriana'," *TAG* 23:16; 24:258.

McCracken, George E., "John Harding of Boreham, Essex" [**Buttolph**], *TAG* 34:205.

Eaton, Arthur Wentworth Hamilton, "Old Boston Families: The **Byles** Family," *NEHGR* 69:101.

Rasmussen, James Anthony, "Ancestry of Robert[1] **Calef** of Boston," *TAG* 66:135.

Woodworth-Barnes, Esther Littleford, "Descendants of Ellis **Callender** of Boston," *NEHGR*, 144:195.

Simons, D. Brenton, "Bigamy in Boston: The Case of Matthew **Cary** and Mary Sylvester," *NEHGR* 159:5.

Lainhart, Ann Smith, "Descendants of Paix **Cazneau**," *NEHGR* 142:126.

Coddington, John Insley, "The Widow Mary Ring, of Plymouth, Mass., and Her Children" [**Clark**], *TAG* 42:201.

Cload see **Buttolph**

Holman, Mary Lovering, "Parentage of John **Cole** of Boston, Mass., and Rhode Island," *NEHGR* 97:194.

Coddington, John Insley, "The Will of Richard **Collacott** of Boston, Mass.," *TAG* 32:92

Hills, Thomas, "The Parentage and English Progenitors of Nathaniel **Coney** of Boston, Mass.," *NEHGR* 61:47.

Coombs see **Barlow**

Barclay, Mrs. John E., "Judith (**Danson)** Wife of Charles **Crossthwayte**," *TAG* 33:232.

Cunningham, Henry Winchester, "Andrew **Cunningham** of Boston and Some of His Descendants," *NEHGR* 55:304.

Barclay, Mrs. John E. and Rachel E., "Elizabeth **Danson** and Her Four Husbands: Warren-Sendall-Hayward-Wilson," *TAG* 47:17.

Montgomery, Robert H., "Humphrey **Davie**, Merchant, of Boston," *TAG* 23:206.

Eaton, Arthur Wentworth Hamilton, "Old Boston Families: The **Deblois** Family," *NEHGR* 67:6.

Holman, Winifred Lovering, "A **Dommett** Family in Boston," *NEHGR* 122:81.

Barclay, Rachel E., "Colonel Thomas⁴ **Doty** of Cape Cod, Plymouth, Boston and Stoughton, Mass." *TAG* 41:20.

Coddington, John Insley, "Francis **Dowse** of Boston and His Ten Daughters," *TAG* 29:161

Anderson, Robert Charles, "The Daughters of Simon¹ **Eire** of Watertown and Boston, Mass." *TAG* 65:17.

Carney, John B., "In Search of **Fayerweather**: The Fayerweather Family of Boston," *NEHGR*, 144:3.

Davis, Walter Goodwin, "The Four Blessing Sisters" [**Firmage**], *TAG* 33:199.

Sprague, Waldo Chamberlain, "Cotton **Flack** of Boston, Mass.," *TAG* 36:223.

Foxe see **Johnson**

Fracker, Stanley Black, "The Descendants of Thomas **Fracker**, Shipbuilder, of Boston," *NEHGR* 124:23.

Franklin see **Davie.**

Belknap, Henry Wycoff, "Some Descendant of Jonathan **Furness** of Boston, Mass.," *NEHGR* 91:396.

Eaton, Arthur Wentworth Hamilton, "Old Boston Families: The Family of Capt. John **Gerrish**," *NEHGR* 67:105.

Hodgman, Arthur Winfred, "The Wife of Thomas **Gilbert** of Boston," *NEHGR* 128:63.

Gording see **Talby**

Greene see **Quincy**

Barclay, Mrs. John E., "Sarah (Jurdain) (Hill) (Sowther) **Greenleaf**," *TAG* 43:14.

Eaton, Arthur Wentworth Hamilton, "Old Boston Families: The **Haliburton** Family," *NEHGR* 71:57.

Harding see **Buttolph**

Harris, Gale Ion, "Arthur[1] Harris of Duxbury, Bridgewater, and Boston, Massachusetts, with an Account of His Apparent Grandson Thomas Harris of Plainfield, Connecticut," *NEHGR* 159:261.

Jones, Roderick Bissell, "**Harrises** in Boston Before 1700," *NEHGR* 105:190.

Harris, Gale Ion, "More **Harrises** of Boston," *NEHGR* 152:313.

Harris, Gale Ion, "James and Sarah (Eliot?) **Harris** of Boston and New London," *NEHGR* 154:3.

Moriarty, G. Andrews, "The **Porter** and **Hawkins** Families of Boston," *TAG* 27:19.

Loeser, Rudolf, "Anthony **Haywood** of Boston," *NEHGR* 153:141.

Hazard see **Johnson**

Barclay, Mrs. John E., "**Hedge-Ingoldsbee-Lothrop** Relationships," *TAG* 34:217.

Phillips, Ralph David and Francis Richmond Sears, "Eliphalet **Hitt** (not Hill) of Boston," *TAG* 27:95.

Jacobus, Donald Lines, "Notes on Connecticut Families-Sir Charles **Hobby** and his Connecticut Descendants," *TAG* 41:135.

Holman, Winifred Lovering, "**Homer–Stevens** Notes, Boston," *TAG* 29:1, 99.

Barclay, Mrs. John E., "Notes on the **Hollingsworth**, Hunter, More, and Woodbury Families of Salem, Mass.," *TAG* 40:79.

Hubbard see **Hobby.**

Wilcox, Wayne Howard Miller, "The Ancestry of Katherine Hamby, Wife of Captain Edward **Hutchinson** of Boston, Massachusetts," *NEHGR* 145:99.

Jackson see **Woodward**

Myers, Marya C. and Donald W. James, Jr., "William[1] **James** of Scituate and Boston, Massachusetts, Shipwright and Quaker," *NEHGR* 155:36.

Thompson, Neil D., "The Parentage of John **Jepson** of Boston, Massachusetts," *TAG* 78:253.

Coddington, John Insley, "Additions and Corrections to the **Jepson** Genealogy," *TAG* 20:85, 173.

Mahler, Leslie, and Melinde Lutz Sanborn, "Mary Foxe, Wife of Lawrence Hazard and Samuel **Johnson** of Stepney, Middlesex, England, and Boston, Massachusetts," *NEHGR* 156:213.

Couet, A.E., "The Ancestry of John **Jones,** 18th Century Boston, Merchant," *NEHGR* 113:216.

Jurdian see **Greenleaf.**

Hunt, John G., "Stebbins-**Keene**-Eldredge, Boston, Massachusetts," *TAG* 41:95.

Holman, Winifred Lovering, "**Kilby** Notes," *TAG* 27:193; 28:34.

Jacobus, Donald Lines, "Deputy-Governor Stephen Goodyear of New Haven, Reverend John Bishop of Stanford, and the **Lake** and **Watts** Families of Boston," *TAG* 16:197.

Peck, S. Allyn, "The English Ancestry of the **Lake** Family of Boston, Massachusetts, and of Sir Edward Lake, Baronet, of England," *TAG* 22:71.

Alger, Arthur M., "The Descendants of Philip and John **Langdon** of Boston," *NEHGR* 30:32.

Hormadey, Mrs. Quinn, "Philip and John **Langdon** of Boston," *NEHGR* 128:48.

Lee, Thomas Amory, "Old Boston Families: The **Lee** Family," *NEHGR* 76:197.

Holman, Winifred Lovering, "**Legare** Notes," *TAG* 25:1.

Wead, Frederick W., "The Second Wife of Hudson[3] **Leverett**," *TAG* 25:160.

Anderson, Robert Charles, John C. Brandon, and Paul C. Reed, "The Ancestry of the Royally Descended **Mansfields** of the Massachusetts Bay," *NEHGR* 155:3.

Wakefield, Robert S., "Elizabeth[3] Thomas, Wife of Joshua[2] **Matson** and Sampson **Moor** of Boston," *TAG* 70:138.

Meakins see **Quincy**

Montgomery, Robert H., "John **Morse** of Boston," *TAG* 24:147.

Mahler, Leslie, "The English Origins of Thomas[1] **Oliver** of Boston," *NEHGR* 157:34.

McTeer, Frances Davis and Frederick C. Warner, "Probable Ancestry of Margaret **Ogilvie** of Boston," *TAG* 41:153.

Coddington, John Insley, "The Descent of the Duke of Montrose, The Prince of Monaco, and Princess Schwarzenberg, From Rev. John **Oxenbridge** of Boston, Mass.," *TAG* 31:60.

Wait, Estelle Wellwood, "The **Papillons** of Boston and Bristol," *NEHGR* 124:161.

Jones, Edson Salisbury, "The Family of George **Parkhurst** of Watertown and Boston, Mass.," *NEHGR* 68:370.

Colket, Meredith, "The **Pelhams** of England and New England-Peter Pelham of Boston, Massachusetts," *TAG* 20:65.

Jacobus, Donald Lines, "The **Phippen** Family and the Wife of Nathan Gold of Fairfield, Connecticut," *TAG* 17:1.

Wead, Frederick W., "Ruth **Pierce's** Five Husbands," *TAG* 26:162.

Place, **Plaice** see **Talby**

Porter see **Hawkins.**

Anderson, Robert Charles, "Michael **Powell** of Dedham and Boston," *NEHGR* 131:173.

Mahler, Leslie, "The English Origins of Edmund[1] **Quincy** of Boston and His Servants, Thomas and Katherine (Greene) Meakins," *NEHGR* 157:31.

Rasmussen, James A., "Edward **Raynsford** of Boston: English Ancestry and American Descendants," *NEHGR*, 139:225.

McCracken, George E., "New Light on Esdras **Reade**, Tailor," *TAG* 28:149.

Nielsen, Donald M., "The **Revere** Family," *NEHGR* 145:291.

Schoeffler, William H., "James **Rogers** of Boston (1729–1793), His Daughter Elizabeth (Rogers) Roby and Their Jepson Link," *TAG* 64:203.

Holman, Mary Lovering, "Notes on Some Immigrants from Ottery St. Mary, Devon – **Salter**," *TAG* 16:132.

Wead, Frederick W., "**Vyall-Sanderson-Sunderland**, Boston, Mass.," *TAG* 37:153.

Woods, Henry Ernest, "Some Descendants of Digory **Sargent** of Boston and Worcester, Mass.," *NEHGR* 58:377.

Articles on Boston Families

Park, Laurence, "Old Boston Families: The **Savage** Family," *NEHGR* 67:198.

Fiske, Jane Fletcher, "The **Sawdy** Family of Boston, Rhode Island, and Points West," *NEHGR*, 148:141.

Sendall see **Danson.**

Sharp see **Ogilvie.**

Barclay, Mrs. John E., "The **Scate-Skeath** Family of Boston; Rebecca, Wife of Ebenezer Allen of Bridgewater," *TAG* 29:87.

Mahler, Leslie, "The English Ancestry of Philip[1] Watson Challis of Ipswich, Massachusetts, with an Account of His Uncle Thomas **Sharpe**, Briefly Resident at Boston, Massachusetts," *TAG* 79:57.

Holman, Winifred Lovering, "The Family of Pilgrim **Simpkins** of Boston," *TAG* 28:87.

Holman, Mary Lovering, "The **Skepper** Family," *TAG* 20:77.

Hansen, James L., "The Ancestry of Joan Legard, Grandmother of the Rev. William[1] **Skepper/Skipper** of Boston, Massachusetts," *TAG* 69:129.

Pitman, H. Minot, "Some **Snellings** of Boston," *NEHGR* 105:54.

Hunt, John G., "Bancroft Addenda with **Sowther** and Gilbert Notes," *TAG* 42:210, 217.

Stebbins see **Keene.**

Stevens see **Homer.**

Sunderland see **Talby**

Sylvester see **Cary**

Hill, Sally Dean Hamblen, "Stephen[2] and Hannah (Place) **Talby** of Boston, Massachusetts, with Notes on Hannah Sunderland Wife of Matthew Armstrong and Abraham Gording of Boston," *TAG* 78:256.

Holman, Winifred Lovering, "Notes-**Thwing**," *TAG* 24:259.

Myers, Marya C., "Tracking Benjamin **Tuell(s)** through Eighteenth-Century Massachusetts and Rhode Island," *TAG* 78:309.

Greene, David L., "The Children of Richard **Tuttle** of Boston," *TAG* 56:143.

Varney, George W., "Thomas **Varney** of Boston and Some of His Descendants," *NEHGR* 149:3.

Wead, Frederick W., "The Wife of Samuel[2] **Vial**," *TAG* 25:159.

Vyall see **Sanderson.**

Willcox, Doris Schreiber, and David Land Willcox, "Double Davenports: Descendants of James and Mary (**Walker**) Davenport of Boston," *NEHGR* 158:5.

Coddington, John Insley, "Robert **Walker** of Boston, Massachusetts," *TAG* 21:58.

Hill, Sally Dean Hamblen, "The Jilting of Samuel **Walker**, Mariner of Boston," *NEHGR* 157:355.

Barclay, Mrs. John E. and Rachel E., "Abigail **Waters**, Wife of Benjamin Walcott," *TAG* 47:159.

Watts see **Lake.**

Barnes, Mrs. W. Carroll, "The Three Wives of David **Webb** of Boston, Mass., and Wethersfield, Conn." *NEHGR* 128:270.

Lainhart, Ann S., "Too Many David **Webbs**," *MD* 50:1.[corrects above article]

Garman, Leo H., "Some Descendants of James **Webster**, Brewer, of Boston, MA," *TAG* 60:41.

Jackson, George West, "Records of the **West** Family of Boston and Taunton, Mass., and Allied Families," *NEHGR* 78:266.

Wilbour, Benjamin Franklin, "The English Ancestry of Samuel **Wilbore** of Boston and William Wilbore of Portsmouth, R.I.," *NEHGR* 112:108.

Montgomery, Robert H., "Nathaniel **Williams** of Boston," *TAG* 28:215.

Bartlett, Joseph Gardner, "Ancestry and Descendants of Rev. John **Wilson** of Boston, Mass.," *NEHGR* 61:36.

Jacobus, Donald Lines, "Seaborn **Wilson** and Shoreborn Wilson of Ipswich and Boston, Massachusetts," *TAG* 35:17.

Wolcott see **Waters.**

Brayton, John Anderson, "From One Boston to Another: Notes on the Ancestry of Mary (Jackson) **Woodward**," *NEHGR* 158:213.

Woodward, Theron Royal, "Nathaniel **Woodward** of Boston, and Some of His Descendants," *NEHGR* 51:169.

Allen, Cameron, "A Virginia Family of Boston: The **Woodwards**," *NEHGR* 115:7.

23 BOSTON AREA REPOSITORIES

L isted here are Boston area repositories, most of which are mentioned in the text of this book. For more information on the collections of these repositories and for information of other repositories, many of which have very specific collections, consult Gregor Trinkaus-Randall, *Massachusetts Special Collections Directory* (Boston, 1999), Marcia D. Melnyk, *Genealogist's Handbook for New England Research* (4th ed., Boston, 1999), and P. William Filby, *Directory of American Libraries with Genealogy or Local History Collections* (Wilmington, Delaware, 1988). Many have published material on their collections, such as the *Guide to the Manuscript Collections of the New England Historic Genealogical Society* (1st ed., Boston, 2002).

American Jewish Historical Society Library
160 Herrick Road, Newton Centre, MA 02459
617-559-8880
www.ajhs.org

Ancient and Honorable Artillery Company of Massachusetts
Armory, Faneuil Hall, Boston, MA 02109
617-227-1638
www.ahacsite.org

Archives of the Archdiocese of Boston
2121 Commonwealth Avenue, Brighton, MA 02135
617-746-5797 (call for an appointment)
www.rcab.org

Boston Athenæum
10½ Beacon Street, Boston, MA 02108
617-227-0270
www.bostonathenaeum.org

Boston City Archives
30 Millstone Road, Hyde Park, MA 02136
617-364-8679 (call for an appointment)
www.cityofboston.gov/archivesandrecords

Boston Public Library
700 Boylston Street, Copley Square, Boston, MA 02117
617-536-5400
www.bpl.org

Boston Police Department — Records Center and Archives
1555 Hyde Park Avenue, Hyde Park, MA 02136
617-343-5166

Boston Registry Archives
Registry Division, Room 213
1 City Hall Square, Boston, MA 02201
617-635-4175 (limited hours)
www.cityofboston.gov/registry

Boston University School of Theology Library (Methodist)
745 Commonwealth Avenue, Boston, MA 02215
617-353-3034
www.bu.edu/sth

The Bostonian Society Library
15 State Street, 3rd floor, Boston, MA 02109
617-720-1713, ext. 12 (call for an appointment)
www.bostonhistory.org

Commonwealth of Massachusetts, Military Division — History Research and Museum
44 Salisbury Street, Worcester, MA 01609
508-797-0334
www.mass.gov/guard/Museum/Information.htm

The Congregational Library and Archives
14 Beacon Street, Boston, MA 02108
617-523-0470
www.14beacon.org

The Diocesan Library and Archives
The Episcopal Diocese of Massachusetts
138 Tremont Street, Boston, MA 02111
617-482-5800
www.diomass.org

Grand Lodge of Masons in Massachusetts Library
186 Tremont Street, Boston, MA 02111
617-426-6040, ext. 4221
www.massfreemasonry.org

Harvard Divinity School
Andover-Harvard Theological Library
45 Francis Avenue, Cambridge, MA 02138
617-495-5788
www.hds.harvard.edu

Hebrew College Library
Rae and Joseph Gann Library
160 Herrick Road, Newton Centre, MA 02459
617-559-8750
www.hebrewcollege.edu

Historic New England
(Formerly Society for the Preservation of New England Antiquities)
141 Cambridge Street, Boston, MA 02114
617-227-3957, ext. 225 or 226 (call for an appointment)
www.historicnewengland.org

Massachusetts Archives
At Columbia Point
220 Morrissey Boulevard, Boston, MA 02125
617-727-2816
www.sec.state.ma.us/arc/arcidx.htm

Massachusetts Historical Society Library
1154 Boylston Street, Boston, MA 02215
617-536-1608
www.masshist.org

Massachusetts Society of Mayflower Descendants
150 Wood Road, Suite 103
Braintree, MA 02184
781-535-6159 (call in advance)
www.massmayflower.org

The National Archives — Northeast Region
Frederick C. Murphy Federal Center
380 Trapelo Road, Waltham, MA 02452
866-406-2379
www.archives.gov/northeast/boston/

New England Historic Genealogical Society Library
101 Newbury Street, Boston, MA 02116-3007
617-536-5740
www.NewEnglandAncestors.org

Registrar of Vital Records and Statistics
150 Mount Vernon Street, 1st floor, Dorchester, MA 02125-3105
617-740-2600
www.state.ma.us/dph/bhsre/rvr/rvr.htm

Society for the Preservation of New England Antiquities
See Historic New England

State Library of Massachusetts
State House, Room 55, Boston, MA 02133
617-727-2595
www.mass.gov/lib/

Suffolk County Probate and Family Court
Edward W. Brooke Courthouse
24 New Chardon Street, 3rd floor, Boston, MA 02114-9660
617-788-8300
www.mass.gov/courts

Suffolk County Registry of Deeds
Edward W. Brooke Courthouse
24 New Chardon Street, 1st floor, Boston, MA 02114-9660
617-788-8575
www.suffolkdeeds.com

University of Massachusetts at Boston
Joseph P. Healey Library
At Columbia Point
100 Morrissey Boulevard, Boston, MA 02125-3393
Boston, MA 02125-3393
617-287-5944
www.lib.umb.edu

Appendix One

MASSACHUSETTS DIVORCE RECORDS
WHERE TO FIND THEM

Roger D. Joslyn

Divorce records are seldom used by genealogical researchers, often because they are assumed to be too modern or restricted. In Massachusetts, divorce records are open for research, and they often contain a great deal of important genealogical information as well as some interesting social and legal history.

The earliest divorces in Massachusetts are 40 known cases for the period 1639 through 1692 when petitions were judged by the county courts, the General Court, and the Court of Assistants (predecessor to the Governor's Council). Details are found in the published Massachusetts Bay and Plymouth Colony records, the published records of the Court of Assistants, and the so-called "Court Files Suffolk" books in the custody of the Clerk of the Supreme Judicial Court (SJC) of Massachusetts [these records are now in the Judicial Archives at the State Archives]. Other information can be found in the Massachusetts Archives [now located on Morrissey Boulevard, Columbia Point]. A list of the 40 cases is in George Elliott Howard, *A History of Matrimonial Institutions* (New York, 1904), 2:333, part of Chapter XV "Divorce in the American Colonies."

Jurisdiction over divorce actions during the period 1692 through 1786 was with the Governor and his Council, although six of the 229 petitions during this period were judged by the legislature from 1755 to 1757. Records are with the Clerk of the SJC, the county courts, and the Massachusetts Archives, and 107 cases for this period are listed in Howard, 2:341-344. Additional cases and information are found in the interesting study by Nancy F. Cott, "Divorce and the Changing Status of Women in Eighteenth-Century Massachusetts," *The William and Mary Quarterly*, 33(1976):586-614.

In 1786 jurisdiction was transferred to the Supreme Judicial Court, and cases are located by using the "Law" dockets (indexes) [now at the Judicial Archives]. After finding the last entry of a divorce action, the file may be requested from the vault using the last docket number. There are dockets for each term (two each year), and even though the indexing is by plaintiff (libelant) only, the divorcing parties will rarely be of different surnames.

The Superior Courts of the Massachusetts counties took over jurisdiction of divorce matters in 1887. Records are usually found with the appropriate county Clerk of Courts, and for most there are indexes in the dockets or in separate volumes (as in Suffolk County). For a list of the records and files and their locations, see Michael S. Hindus, *The Records of the Massachusetts Superior Court And Its Predecessors: An Inventory and Guide* (Boston) 1977.

Since 1922, the county probate courts have had concurrent jurisdiction of divorce actions, and most divorces from that date have been judged in that court. In at least Suffolk County there is a separate office of the probate court for divorce records, whereas in other counties divorces are kept with other probate files. For Massachusetts divorces from 1952, there is a statewide index maintained in the Registry of Vital Records and Statistics [150 Mt. Vernon St., Dorchester, MA]. This index shows the names of the couple, the year, the county and the case file number. There are no actual divorce records in the Vital Records office, the index is not often updated, and many of the case numbers have been found to be incorrectly entered.

The information found in a divorce record varies considerably in the earlier records. Some petitions are very brief, while others may contain much detail and several depositions from persons providing information or character references. Since there are no published lists of Massachusetts divorces for the period beginning 1786, a search of the "Law" dockets in the SJC can be tedious, unless the approximate year is known. The dockets of the SJC, and later for the county superior courts, show the names of the libel(ant) and libelee, and some brief record of actions taken, such as the date a summons was served or the date of a final (nisi) decree.

From 1922, when the county probate courts began to hear divorce cases, there is more uniformity in the case files. A petition for divorce will identify the parties, when and where they were married, places and dates of residence as a married couple, and a brief statement (without detail) of the reason a divorce is being sought. If minor children are involved, their names and dates of birth (or ages) are also given. There may be copies of a summons and other court papers and perhaps a copy of the marriage certificate, and if a divorce is granted, it will be noted together with such conditions as custody of minor children. If both parties file for divorce, the records may be found in separate files.

Finally, many divorces of Massachusetts residents were not granted in the Commonwealth, and one must look in other states, and countries, for that information.

APPENDIX TWO

MINISTERS IN BOSTON UP TO 1846
Compiled by Neil Todd

ABBOTT, John Lovejoy
   First Church, Unitarian

ADAMS, Nehemiah
   Union/Essex St.Church, Trinitarian

ADAMS, Thomas C.
   West Universalist Society

AIKEN, Silas
   Park St. Church, Trinitarian

ALLEN, James
   First Church, Unitarian

ALVORD, John W.
   Phillip's Church, Trinitarian

ANNAN, Robert
   Federal St. Church, Unitatian

APPLETON, William, Esq.
   St. Stephen's Church, Episcopal

ARCHER, Armstrong
   African Baptist Church

BACON, John
   Old South Church, Trinitarian

BAILEY, John
   First Church, Unitarian

BALDWIN, Thomas
   Second Baptist Church

BALL, Harvey
   Second Baptist Church

BALLOU, Hosea
   Second Universalist Church

BANVARD, Joseph
   Harvard St. Church, Baptist

BARNARD, Charles F.
   Pitts St. Church, Unitarian
   Warren St. Chapel, Unitarian

BARRETT, Samuel
   Chambers St. Church, Unitarian

BARTOL, Cyrus A.
   West Church, Unitarian

BEECHER, Edward
   Park St. Church, Trinitarian
   Salem St. Church, Trinitarian

BEECHER, Lyman
   Bowdoin St. Church, Trinitarian

BELKNAP, Jeremy
   Federal St. Church, Unitarian

BEMAN, Jeheil C.
   Zion Church, Methodist

BIGELOW, Andrew
   Pitts St. Chapel, Unitarian

BLACK, George H.
   African Baptist Church

BLACK, William
   First Methodist Episcopal Church

BLAGDEN, George W.
Old South Church, Trinitarian
Salem St. Church, Trinitarian

BLAIKIE, Alexander
First Presbytarian Church

BLAIR, Samuel
Old South Church, Trinitarian

BLAKE, J.L.
St. Matthew's Church, Episcopal

BLOOD, Caleb
Third Baptist Church

BOIES, Artemas
Pine St. Church, Trinitarian

BOSWORTH, G.W.
South Baptist Church

BOAND, Ephraim
Second Baptist Church

BOWEN, Penuel
New South Church, Unitarian

BRIDGE, Jonathan D.
First Methodist Episcopal Church

BRIDGE, Thomas
First Church, Unitarian

BROCKWELL, Charles
King's Chapel, Unitarian

BROWN, John
Pine St. Church, Trinitarian

BUCKMINSTER, J.S.
Brattle St. Church, Unitarian

BURNHAM, Edwin
First Christian Church

BURTON, Warren
Pitts St. Chapel

BUTLER, Clement M.
Grace Church, Episcopal

BYLES, Mather
Hollis St. Church, Unitarian

BYLES, Mather Jr.
Christ Church, Episcopal

CALLENDER, Elisha
First Baptist Church

CALLENDER, Ellis
First Baptist Church

CALLION, C.W.
Church of St. Nicholas, Catholic

CANER, Henry
King's Chapel, Unitarian

CAPEN, Lemuel
Dawes' Place Church, Unitarian

CARROLL, Bishop
Church of the Holy Cross, Catholic

CARY, Samuel
King's Chapel, Unitarian

CHANNING, William E.
Federal St. Church, Unitarian

CHAPIN, E.H.
Second Universalist Church

CHAPMAN, William R.
Layden/Green St. Church, Trinitarian
First Free Church, Trinitarian

CHAUNCY, Charles
First Church, Unitarian

CHECKLEY, Samuel
New South Church, Unitarian

CHECKLEY, Samuel Jr.
Second Church, Unitarian

CHRISTIAN, Washington
African Baptist Church

CHURCH, Pharcellus
Bowdoin Square Baptist Church

CLARK, Robert
King's Chapel, Unitarian

CLARK, Thomas M.
Trinity Church, Episcopal
Grace Church, Episcopal

CLARKE, J.F.
Church of the Disciples, Unitarian

CLARKE, John
First Church, Unitarian

CLAY, Joseph
First Baptist Church

CLEVERLY, A.P.
Universalist Free Church

CLINCH, Joseph H.
St. Matthew's Church, Episcopal

CLOUGH, Simon
First Christian Church

COBB, Sylvanus
Sixth Universalist Church

COFFIN, E.W.
South Universalist Society

COLMAN, Benjamin
Brattle St. Church, Unitarian

COLVER, Nathaniel
South Baptist Church
Tremont St. Baptist Church

CONDY, Jeremiah
First Baptist Church

CONOLLY, Horace L.
St. Matthew's Church, Episcopal

COOK, T.D.
Fourth Universalist Society

COOLIDGE, James I.T.
Purchase St. Church, Unitarian

COOPER, Samuel
Brattle St. Church, Unitarian

COOPER, William
Brattle St. Church, Unitarian

COTTON, John
First Church, Unitarian

CRESSY, Timothy R.
South Baptist Church

CROSWELL, William
Christ Church, Episcopal
Church of the Advent, Episcopal

CRUDDEN, Peter
Church of the Holy Cross, Catholic

CRUFT, Samuel B.
Suffolk St.Chapel, Unitarian

CUMMING, Alexander
Old South Church, Trinitarian

CUSHMAN, R.W.
Bowdoin Square Baptist Church

CUTLER, Timothy
Christ Church, Episcopal

DAVENPORT, Addington
King's Chapel, Unitarian
Trinity Church, Episcopal

DAVENPORT, John
First Church, Unitarian

DAVIS, John
Second Baptist Church

DEAN, Paul
First Universalist Church
Bulfinch St. Society, Unitarian

DeCHEVERUS, John L.
Church of the Holy Cross, Catholic

DEGEN, Henry W.
Fifth Methodist Episcopal Church

DENNIS, Joseph S.
Fifth Universalist Society

DENNISON, C.W.
Methodist Protestant Church

DOANE, George W.
Trinity Church, Episcopal

DRIVER, Thomas
South Baptist Church

DUNBAR, Duncan
South Baptist Church

DWIGHT, Moseley
Richmond St. Church, Methodist

DWIGHT, Sereno E.
Park St. Church, Trinitarian

EASTBURN, Manton
Trinity Church, Episcopal
Church of the Messiah, Episcopal

EATON, Asa
Christ Church, Episcopal
St. Stephen's Church, Episcopal

ECK, J.
Church of the Holy Trinity, Catholic

ECKLEY, Joseph
Old South Church, Trinitarian

EDMONDS, Edmond
First Christian Church

EDWARDS, Justin
Salem St. Church, Trinitarian

ELIOT, Andrew
New North Church, Unitarian

ELIOT, John
New North Church, Unitarian

EMBLEM, John
First Baptist Church

EMERSON, Edward
Second Church, Unitarian

EMERSON, Oliver
First Church, Unitarian

EVERETT, Edward
Brattle St. Church, Unitarian

EVERETT, Oliver
New South Church, Unitarian

FAIRCHILD, Joy H.
Phillip's Church, Trinitarian
Parson Church, Trinitarian

FENWICK, Benedict
Church of the Holy Cross, Catholic
St. Mary's Church, Catholic
St. Patrick's Church, Catholic

FINNEY, C.G.
First Free Church, Trinitarian

FITCH, Charles
First Free Church, Trinitarian

FITZPATRICK, J.B.
Church of the Holy Cross, Catholic

FITZSIMMONS, Terence
Church of St. Peter and St. Paul,
Catholic

FLOOD, Patrick
Church of the Holy Cross, Catholic
St. Mary's Church, Catholic

FORMAN, J.G.
South Universalist Society

FOSDICK, David
Hollis St. Church, Unitarian

FOX, Thomas B.
Warren St. Congregational Church,
Unitarian

FOXCROFT, Thomas
First Church, Unitarian

FRANKLIN, Thomas L.
St. John's Church, Episcopal

FREEMAN, Thomas L.
King's Chapel, Unitarian

FROTHINGHAM, Nathaniel L.
First Church, Unitarian

GAIR, Thomas
Second Baptist Church

GANNETT, Ezra S.
Federal St. Church, Unitarian

GARDNIER, John S.J.
Trinity Church, Episcopal

GEE, Joshua
Second Church, Unitarian

GREENLEAF, Jonathan
Mariner's Church, Trinitarian

GIVEN, John
African Baptist Church

GOFF, Isaac C.
First Christian Church

GOOCH, Samuel
African Baptist Church

GOULD, Thomas
First Baptist Church

GRAVES, Hiram A.
East Boston Baptist Church

GRAVES, Joseph M.
East Boston Baptist Church

GRAY, Ellis
Second Church, Unitarian

GRAY, Frederick T.
Bulfinch St. Church, Unitarian
Pitts St. Chapel, Unitarian

GREATON, James
Christ Church, Episcopal

GREEN, Samuel
Union/Essex St. Church, Trinitarian

GREENWOOD, F.W.P.
King's Chapel, Unitarian
New South Church, Unitarian

GRIFFIN, Edward D.
Park St. Church, Trinitarian

GROSVENOR, Cyrus
First Baptist Church

HAGUE, William
First Baptist Church
Federal St. Baptist Church

HAMIL, M.
Church of St. Peter and St. Paul,
Catholic

HARDY, Richard B.
Church of the Holy Cross, Catholic

HARRIS, Henry
King's Chapel, Unitarian

HASKELL, Samuel
Christ Church

HASKINS, George F.
Church of the Holy Cross, Catholic

HATCH, W.H.
First M.E. Church, Episcopal

HATTON, George
King's Chapel, Unitarian

HAWES, Prince
Phillip's Church, Trinitarian

HEMPSTEAD, Henry E.
Sixth Methodist Episcopal Church

HICHBORN, Alexander
Sixth Universalist Church

HIGGINS, Samuel H.
Second Methodist Church

HIMES, J.V.
First Christian Church
Chardon St. Church, Christian

HITCHCOCK, Robert
Maverick Church, Trinitarian

HOLLEY, Horace
Hollis St. Church, Unitarian

HOLMAN, J.W.
Free Will Baptist Church

HOOPER, William
Trinity Church, Episcopal
West Church, Unitarian

HOPKINS, John H.
Trinity Church, Episcopal

HOWARD, Simeon
West Church, Unitarian

HOWARD, Thomas
King's Chapel, Unitarian

HOWE, Joseph
New South Church, Unitarian

HOWE, William
Friend St. Baptist Church

HULL, Isaac
First Baptist Church

HUNT, John
Old South Church, Trinitarian

HUNTINGTON, Frederick D.
South Congregation Church,
Unitarian

HUNTINGTON, Joshua
Old South Church, Trinitarian

IDE, George B.
Federal St. Baptist Church

JACKSON, ——
South Baptist Church

JARVIS, Samuel Farmer
St. Paul's Church, Episcopal

JENKS, William
Layden/Green St. Church, Trinitarian

JOHNES, Abner
First Christian Church

JOHNSON, Henry
Second African Methodist Episcopal
Church

KEMPE, George J.
German Evangelical, German
Protestant

KING, T.S.
Hollis St. Church, Unitarian

KIRK, Edward N.
Mount Vernon Church, Trinitarian

KIRKLAND, John T.
New South Church, Unitarian

KNOWLES, James D.
Second Baptist Church

KROES, P.P.
St. Mary's Church, Catholic

LANDON, George
Fourth Methodist Episcopal Church

La POTERIE, M.
Church of the Holy Cross

LATHROP, John
Second Church, Unitarian

LEWIS, Stephen
Christ Church, Episcopal

LINSLEY, Joel H.
Park St. Church, Trinitarian

LIPPITT, George W.
Dawes' Place Church, Unitarian

LORD, Daniel M.
Mariner's Church, Trinitarian

LOTHROP, S.K.
Brattle St. Church, Unitarian

LOVELL, Stephen
Second Methodist Church

LOWELL, Charles
West Church, Unitarian

LYNCH, Thomas
St. Patrick's Church, Catholic

LYNDON, P.F.
Church of the Holy Cross, Catholic

MALCOLM, Howard
Federal St. Baptist Church

MANAHAN, A.
Church of the Holy Cross, Catholic

MANSON, Charles
Grace Church, Episcopal

MARTIN, P.
Church of the Holy Trinity, Catholic

MATHER, Dr.
First Universalist Church

MATHER, Cotton
Second Church, Unitarian

MATHER, Increase
Second Church, Unitarian

MATHER, Samuel
Second Church, Unitarian

MATIGNON, F.A.
Church of the Holy Cross, Catholic

MAYHEW, Jonathan
West Church, Unitarian

MAYO, John
Second Church, Unitarian

McBURNEY, Samuel
Grace Church, Episcopal
St. Stephen's Church, Episcopal

McELROY, R.R.J.
St. Mary's Church, Catholic

McGRATH, G.
Free Church, Catholic

McGUIRE, James
Church of the Holy Cross, Catholic

McMAHON, J.B.
Free Church, Catholic

MEAD, Zechariah
Grace Church, Episcopal

MERRILL, A.D.
Third Methodist Episcopal Church

MILES, John
First Baptist Church

MILES, Samuel
King's Chapel, Unitarian

MINER, A.A.
Second Universalist Church

MITCHELL, Edward
First Universalist Church

MONTAGUE, William
Christ Church, Episcopal

MOODY, J.
First Church, Unitarian

MOOREHEAD, John
Federal St. Church, Unitarian

MORGREDGE, Charles
First Christian Curch

MOTT, Darius
South Universalist Society

MOTT, Melish
South Congregational Church, Unitarian

MURRAY, John
First Universalist Church

NAYLOR, ——
South Baptist Church

NEAL, Rollin H.
First Baptist Church
South Baptist Church

NEWELL, William W.
Maverick Church, Trinitarian

NORTON, John
First Church, Unitarian

NOTT, Handel G.
Federal St. Baptist Church

NOYES, E.
Free Will Baptist Church

O'BRIEN, Nicholas
Church of St. Nicholas, Catholic

O'REILLY, James
Church of the Holy Cross, Catholic
St. Mary's Church, Catholic

OVIATT, George A.
Suffolk St. Union Church, Trinitarian

OXENBRIDGE, John
First Church, Unitarian

PALFREY, John G.
Brattle St. Church, Unitarian

PARKER, Samuel
Trinity Church, Episcopal

PARKMAN, Francis
New North Church, Unitarian

PATTON, William W.
Phillip's Church, Trinitarian

PAUL, Thomas
African Baptist Church

PEABODY, Ephraim
King's Chapel, Unitarian

PEIRCE, B.K.
Canton St. Church, Methodist

PEIRCE, Thomas C.
Third Methodist Episcopal Church

PEMBERTON, Ebenezer
Second Church, Unitarian
Old South Church, Trinitarian

PHELPS, Amos A.
Pine St. Church, Trinitarian
First Free Church, Trinitarian
Maverick Church, Trinitarian

PHELPS, Austin
Pine St. Church, Trinitarian

PIERPONT, John
Hollis St. Church, Unitarian

PLATHE, ——
Church of the Holy Trinity, Catholic

PLUMB, D.H.
West Universalist Society

PORTER, James
First Methodist Episcopal Church

POTTER, Alonzo
St. Paul's Church, Episcopal

PRICE, Roger
King's Chapel, Unitarian
Trinity Church, Episcopal

PRINCE, Thomas
Old South Church, Trinitarian

RANDALL, George M.
Church of the Messiah, Episcopal

RATCLIFFE, Robert
King's Chapel, Unitarian

RAYMOND, J.T.
African Baptist Church

RAYMOND, Miner
Third Methodist Episcopal Church

REMINGTON, Stephen
Second Methodist Church

RICE, William
Fourth Methodist Episcopal Church

RICHARDS, George
Central Church, Trinitarian

RIPLEY, George
Purchase St. Church, Unitarian

ROBBINS, Chandler
Second Church, Unitarian

ROBINSON, John P.
Seamen's Chapel, Episcopal

ROGERS, William M.
Central Church, Trinitarian

RUDBALL, Abel
Christ Church, Episcopal

RUDGE, Christopher
King's Chapel, Unitarian

RUSSELL, John
First Baptist Church

RUSSELL, P.R.
Third Christian Church

RUSSELL, William P.
First Free Church, Trinitarian

SABINE, James
Union/Essex St. Church, Trinitarian

SANFORD, Miles
East Boston Baptist Church

SARGENT, John T.
Suffolk St. Chapel, Unitarian

SCHMIDT, Frederick
German Lutheran

SCUDDER, Moses L.
Fourth Methodist Episcopal Church

SEWELL, Joseph
Old South Church, Trinitarian

SHACKFORD, Charles C.
Dawe's Place Church, Unitarian

SHARP, Daniel
Third Baptist Church

SKILLMAN, Isaac
Second Baptist Church

SKINNER, Otis A.
Fifth Universalist Church

SKINNER, Thomas
Pine St. Church, Trinitarian

SMITH, Amos
New North Church, Unitarian

SMITH, Elias
First Christian Church

SMITH, M.H.
Pilgrim Society, Trinitarian

SNOWDEN, Samuel
African Methodist Episcopal Society

STARKWEATHER, John
First Free Church, Trinitarian

STEARNS, Samuel H.
Old South Church, Trinitarian

STILLMAN, Samuel
First Baptist Church

STONE, John S.
St. Paul's Church, Episcopal

STOW, Phineas
Boston Baptist Bethel

STOWE, Baron
Second Baptist Church

STREETER, Sebastian
First Universalist Church

TAYLOR, E.T.
Bethel Church, Methodist

THACHER, Samuel C.
New South Church, Unitarian

THATCHER, Peter
Brattle St. Church, Unitarian
New North Church, Unitarian

THAYER, John
Church of the Holy Cross, Catholic

THOMAS, Moses G.
Broadway Church, Unitarian

THOMPSON, J.S.
First Christian Church

TOWNE, Jos. H.
Leyden/Green St. Church, Trinitarian

TROUTBEE, A.M.
King's Chapel, Unitarian

TURNBULL, Robert
Harvard St. Church, Baptist

VINTON, Alex. H.
St. Paul's Church, Episcopal

WADSWORTH, Benj.
First Church, Unitarian

WAINWRIGHT, Jonthan M.
Trinity Church, Episcopal

WALDRON, William
Second Church, Unitarian

WALTER, William
Christ Church, Episcopal
Trinity Church, Episcopal

WARE, Henry Jr.
Second Church, Unitarian

WATERBURY, J.W.
Bowdoin St. Church, Trinitarian

WATERSTON, Robert C.
Pitts St. Chapel
Church of the Savior, Unitarian

WATSON, John L.
Trinity Church, Episcopal

WAYLAND, Francis
First Baptist Church

WEBB, John
New North Church, Unitarian

WELLS, E.M.P.
St. Stephens Church, Episcopal

WELSTEAD, William
Second Church, Unitarian

WEST, Samuel
Hollis St. Church, Unitarian

WHITMAN, Joseph
Fifth Methodist Church

WHITTEMORE, Benj.
Fourth Universalist Church

WIGHT, Ebenezer
Hollis St. Church, Unitarian

WILLARD, Samuel
Old South Church, Trinitarian

WILSON, John
First Church, Unitarian

WINCHELL, James M.
First Baptist Church

WINSLOW, Hubbard
Bowdoin St. Church, Trinitarian

WISNER, Benj. B.
Old South Church, Trinitarian

WOART, John
Christ Church, Episcopal

WORCESTER, Thomas
New Jerusalem Church

YOUNG, Alexander
New South Church, Unitarian

APPENDIX THREE

THE HOME FOR DESTITUTE CATHOLIC CHILDREN

Ann S. Lainhart

Last summer, [1985] the Archives of the Archdiocese of Boston received the records of the Home for Destitute Catholic Children. The Home is now known as Nazareth, and while it closed its doors as a residential facility in 1985, it still continues to provide foster care and other child services. The records of this Home are going to be a very important source of information on Catholic families in Boston in the nineteenth and twentieth centuries and will provide names and information on many children who were sent west on the orphans' trains. These records begin in 1864 and continue well into the twentieth century. The pre-1900 records can be used with relatively few restrictions and they are the subject of this article. The later records have more restrictions that can be explained by the Archives staff. When looking at these records, it quickly becomes apparent that this Home was not simply an orphanage; often one or both of the parents of these children were dead, but in the majority of the cases both parents were living. Instead, this was a temporary home for children from families who could not take care of them; it is not uncommon to see two or three children with the same surname being admitted on the same day. It was rare for a child to remain here for more than a few months.

The first three registers are from 5 July 1864 to 19 October 1901, and have only one small gap in early 1884. In these thirty-eight years, the Home handled 18,263 children. These registers are indexed by first letter of the surname. The books themselves have the following categories printed across the top of the pages: Number; Names of children; Age, Yrs, Mos; Sex; Date of Admission; Names of Parents; Residences of Parents; Nativity of Parents; Date of Leaving; To Whom and Where Sent; Remarks. After the names of the parents, the childrens' condition is usually noted: dead, arrested, intemperate, ill, etc. The nativity of the parents often gives town of birth in this country or county of birth in Ireland. To Whom and Where Sent usually just notes that a parent or relative took the child, but it also notes non-related families with whom the child was placed, often for adoption (though the information on adoption is little more than the name of the family that took the child). Remarks generally indicate how the children came to the home. They were often sent by the local parish or by the Society for Prevention of Cruelty to Children, but sometimes a neighbor brought them in. Some examples of the information given about the children include a three-year-old girl who was admitted because her mother was in the hospital and her father had deserted the family. She remained for three months before her mother could take her back. Then there was an eleven-year-old boy sent from St. James parish to be adopted. He was admitted on 30 July 1879, when his father was dead and his mother was in the hospital. His mother died on 15 October 1879 and the boy "absconded" from the Home on 14 November. In a third example a five year, 6-month-old boy was brought in by an agent for the Society for Prevention of Cruelty to Children, to be admitted for the third time. Both parents are listed as arrested and he was taken back by his mother after one month.

For years I have heard about "orphan's" trains that took children "out west" from Boston; these records present the first concrete information I have seen on children leaving Boston. I have put orphan in quotation marks, because as mentioned above, most of these children were not orphans, including those who were sent on the trains and were later often adopted by the families with whom they were placed. These records show that children were sent from Boston to Yankton, Union, Lake, and Clay counties in Dakota; Allamakee, Linn, Gutherie, Cherokee, and Woodbury counties in Iowa; Platte and Cedar counties in Nebraska; Hennepin & Scott counties in Minnesota; Northumberland county in Pennsylvania; Erie county in New York; and Charles county in Maryland. For example, these records show that in 1883 and early 1884, four groups of children were sent to Reverend George Sheehan in Welshtown, Yankton County, Dakota. They were sent on 22 July 1883, 4 September 1883, 16 December 1883, and 26 May 1884. In many cases, the names of the families in Yankton, Union, Lake, and Clay counties with whom a child was placed are given.

These records are a very important source for information on Catholic families in nineteenth-century Boston, but they should also prove invaluable for descendants of people who appear in one of the Dakotas or Iowa or Nebraska in the 1900 census, as born in Massachusetts. It just may be that they were sent out on one of the orphans' trains from Boston. If so, relatives may still live in New England. I searched these records for a client's grandmother. The most likely candidate for her grandmother was admitted to the Home with her brother in 1883; both their parents were listed as intemperate. The 1880 census showed that these two children had three siblings; two old enough by 1883 to be on their own, and one who would have been only four in 1883 and may have remained with the mother. Both of the children admitted to the Home were sent to Dakota on 16 December 1883. Therefore, it is very likely that there are descendants of the other siblings and they may possibly still be in the Boston area.

APPENDIX FOUR

BOSTON RECORD COMMISSIONERS REPORTS

Ann S. Lainhart

The following information on the *Boston Record Commissioners Reports* is reprinted with permission of *The Essex Genealogist* from my article published in August 1999 (19:131-4).

Anyone researching their ancestors in Boston in the seventeenth, eighteenth, and early nineteenth centuries is familiar with the four volumes of the Record Commissioners Reports that have the town's vital records, but probably few have delved into the other thirty-five volumes. These have minutes of the town meetings, selectmen's meetings, tax lists, Aspinwall Notarial Records, and miscellaneous items. A few of these volumes also have records of Charlestown, Dorchester, and Roxbury, towns that are now part of Boston. The biggest drawback to using these other volumes is that they are mostly indexed by surname only. If you are dealing with one of the larger families in Boston, this can mean a lot of pages to check! But I encourage you to do so. With so many New England town records not in print, or only on microfilm in the old handwriting, or not even yet microfilmed, these published Boston records should not be overlooked by anyone with Boston ancestry.

As with most town records, you may not find the answers to genealogical questions, like who was John's father or what was Mary's maiden name, but you may find some very interesting biographical details which will help you to understand how your ancestors lived. Here are some random examples; the first three are from minutes of the selectmen's meetings and the last three from minutes of town meetings:

> 11 Jan 1765. Mr Langdon Usher at the North Grammar School being still con-
> fined to his House by means of Bodily disorder the Select men this Day Agreed

with Mr Andrew Eliot Junr to serve the school in that capacity for one Month.

17 Jun 1767. Thomas Littlewood (?), from London last from Philadelphia came ye 19. of April last appeared and asked liberty of the Selectmen to open a Shop in this Town adjoining The Probate Office for the carrying on the business of a Silk Dyer - whereupon Voted, that he have liberty.

14 Sep 1768. Mr Paul Farmer was directed to receive into the Alms house by two of the Selectmen - vizt - Joseph Jackson & John Ruddock, to be supported there at the public charge one Richard Swansbury, a Stranger & not an Inhabitant of any Town in this Province nor having wherewithall to support himself.

2 Feb 1779. The Committee of seven appointed, to Enquire into the Conduct of Forestallers Engrossers and Monopolizers, and to ascertain Facts - Reported in part: That one Sampson Reed a Stranger is suspected of Engrossing and Forestalling the Necessaries of Life - that in a particular Manner he has monopolized a great quantity of Glass.

12 Mar 1798. What steps shall be taken to prevent dead Carcasses being thrown into the Mill Pond - was read - whereupon moved & Voted, that Honble Thomas Dawes Esq., William Cooper, John Warren Esq., William Eustis Esq., a Committee relative to Health be a Committee to consider & Report thereon.

9 Apr 1804. The Request of William Tudor, Harrison G. Otis and Jonathan Mason Esquires, "that the Town will appoint Agents to treat with them upon the terms, on which they may obtain the whole or part of the Town's Land on Orange Street now occupied by Capt Nathl Curtis for the purpose of building the proposed New Bridge therefrom."

Then to show what can be found when following one family, I culled out the following material on the Gillam family in the seventeenth century. It shows that Benjamin Gillam was an early shipwright and owned parts of more than one ship, that he served the town, owned land with a house and wharfe, probably had a son Benjamin since they are called junior and senior, and may be related to a Robert and an Edward Gillam. This material comes from seven of the Reports volumes and I have put them all into one chronological list:

1637   25 Sep Also Robert Gillam, marryner, hath leave to buy a house plott where he can.

        8 Jan   The great Allottments at Rumley Marsh and Pullen Point. 8. Beniamyn Gillam, eight and twenty acrs: bounded on the South with Thomas Matson; on the West with Mr Keine; and on the North with John Gallopp; and on the East with the highway.

1638   16 Apr Also that all fence about the Corne feilds shalbe sufficiently made, according to Court order...And to be seene unto by these men...Beniamyn Gillam.

1639   25 Mar   Also it is ordered that all the Cornefeild fences about the Towne shalbe made sufficient before the eight day of this next 2d moneth...about the fort feild by or brethren Beniamyn Gillam.

1640   30 Mar   ...and likewise Beniamin Gillam and Edmund Jackson for the Fort field.

   20 Apr   23. John Odline is to have 8 Acres of marsh at muddie River for L4...Ben. Gillum 10 Acrs for L5.

1645   10 Dec   A bond of 1000ii wherein Adam Winthrop & Benjamin gillom are bound to Emanuel Downeing Joshua ffoote Stephen Winthrop & Thomas Bell to prepare 100 Masts of white pine or spruise.

1646   1 Dec   An Attest to a Copie of a Bill of sale of one fourth part of the Unity of Boston wththappurtenances from Benjamin Gillom to John Leverit.

1647   23 Aug   Mr Adam Winthrop constitued Isaac Allerton of New haven his Attnr to aske &c: a debt of twelve pounds sterl payable in Bever to himself & Benjamin Gillom.

   23 Sep   Benjamin Gillam ordered Thomas Bell to pay his Bills of Exchange to John Parke or his assignes out of the pduce of his pt of the Cargo.

   30 Oct   I testifyed under my hand a Copie of a Bill of sale of so much as comes to two hundrd & fifty pounds of the Ship Expectation & her Cargo, from John Turner & Benjamin Gillom to Stephen & Adam Winthrop.

1648   Benjamin Gillom his possession within the limits of Boston. One house and garden bounded with Benjamin Ward on the west; Mr Wm Hibbins south; John Compton and the Cove east; and the marsh north. Also one house and lott bounded with Wm Deming westward and northward; Robert Turners pasture east; and the lane southeast.

   12 Mar   ...likewise if Mr Benjamin Gellom doe buy a new ship at the south ward & shall require the service of the sd Bullocke, to pceed as Master then the sd Bullock is not to refuse...

26 Mar There is graunted unto...Benia: Gillum...liberty to make a highway from their howses over the marsh to the bridge.

12 May Wm King constituted Benjamin Gillom his Atturney to receive his wages due from Mr Robt Risby & Mr Tho: Gainer.

1649 15 Apr I Joseph Armitage do acknowledge my selfe indebted to Benjamin Gillom...the said Joseph Armitage is to cloth Benjamin Gillom from the knee upward wth a convenient suite of apparell & a Bever hatt wth in one month...

1650 25 Jul I attested that Mr ffrancis Willoughbie is one of or Magistrates & Arthur Gill & Benjamin Gillom two able Ship Carpenters.

1657 28 Jul Ben. Gillam is fined ten shillings for making a fire upon the wharfe.

22 Mar Ben. Gillam hath five shillings abated of his fine for heating a pitch pott on the wharfe.

1665 1 Sep Mr Benjamine Gillum Jr haueing obstructed the high way leading to Fort hill, one the West side of his dwelling house and ware house, Itt is therefore ordered that the sd highe way shall be forth with layed open & left 10 foot in bredth vpon penaltie of 20s a week weekly vpon the defect there of.

1668 27 Apr Libertie is granted to Capt Benjn Gillam to wharfe before his owne ground adjoyninge to his dwelling house.

1672/3 10 Mar Water Bayliffes - John Anderson & Benjamin Gillam

1673 31 Mar Wee whose names are underwritten doe each of us... promise to...begin & carry an end the wall or wharfe as within mentioned: Joseph Gillam

1673/4 16 Mar Water Bayliffs - John Anderson & Benjamin Gillam

1676 Tax list: Benjamine Gillam and Joseph Gillam

1680 2 Dec I, Benjamine Gillam, senr, of Bostone doe binde myselfe unto Capt. Tho. Brattle Treas. of Sd towne that William Wharton, block maker, Shall not be Chargeable to the Sd towne.

1685 The Original draught of the Rates in Capt. Hutchinsons

and Capt. Townsends Compa Ano 1685: Mr Turfery at Mrs. Gillams.

1687	Tax list: Benj. Gillam
1688	Tax list: Benja Gillam
1691	Tax list: Benjamen Gillam
1695	Tax list: Benjamin Gillam
1701/2 2 Mar	Peter Barber's List of Abatemts: Edward Gilam
1701/2 9 Mar	Capt Benja Gillam is chosen Constable
1707 3 Apr	Approbation of the Majr part of the Justices within the Town of Boston for the setting up of Timber houses and Buildings within the said Town: To Samuel Phillips to Erect a Building with Timber for a Salt House...on his Wharfe, which he hath lately built on the fflatts before the Land which was formerly the Land of Capt. Benjamin Gillam dec'd.

APPENDIX FIVE

INVENTORY OF THE ESTATE OF AMASA DAVIS

Amasa Davis was born at Woodstock, Connecticut, April 17, 1744; died at Boston, January 30, 1825, age 80 and was the son of Joshua and Sarah (Pierrepont) Davis. He married Sarah Whitney, who died at Boston, August 13, 1794 age 46 or 47.

He was a merchant and distiller. He became a member of the Ancient and Honorable Artillery Company in 1786 and was made Quartermaster General of Massachusetts in 1787 which position he held until his death. His total estate included $45,000.00 in real estate, $4,100.00 in stocks and turnpike shares, and $500 for a pew in the Hollis Street Church. With the following personal estate, his estate was worth $50,333.71 (Suffolk County Probate #27487, 123:192).

Front Parlour

1 Portrait of the Deceased $50.00

1 Portrait of Washington 10.00

1 Brussels Carpet 30.00

1 Sofa 5.00

1 pair Card Tables 6.00

12 Fancy Chairs @ 1.50 18.00

2 Foot Stools @.75 1.50

1 pair Looking Glasses @16 32.00

1 pair Mirrors @12 24.00

1 Backgammon Board & Loo? Box 3.00

1 Fender & Grate 5.00 $184.50

Front Entry

1 Set Dining Tables 20.00

1 Hat Stand
1 Stair Carpet & 38 Rods

Dining Room
    1 Kidminster Carpet
    1 Hearth Rugg
    1 Side Board
    3 Mahogany Knife Cases
    12 Fancy Chairs
    1 Mahogany Breakfast Table
    1 Large Looking Glass
    1 pair Side Lamps
    1 pair Card Racks
    Shovel Tongs & Hooks & Poker
    Fender Bellows & Brush
    Large Bible 2 vol.
    Grate & Blower
    4 pair Boots & 2 pair Shoes
    1 Stove
    1 Eight day Clock
    1 old Desk
    1 Watch
    1 Boule Quicksilver

Middle Uper Chamber
    1 Field Bedstead Bed Bolster & Pillows
    1 Single Bedstead Mattress & Bolsters
    1 trunk Bed Clothes Contg. 14 Blankets
    1 trunk Contg. Bed Curtains & Coverings
    1 Traveling trunk
    2 Bureaux
    1 Cradle
    6 Chairs
    9 Chairs
    Mahogany Screen
    1 pair gilt framed Looking Glasses
    1 Mahogany framed Looking Glass
    2 pair Andirons Shovels & Tongs
    1 low post Bedstead
    Bed & window Cornices
    1 Large Trunk Contg. Saddle Cloth & Portmanteau

East Uper Chamber
    1 Mahogany Bedstead Bed & Bolster
    16 Jelly Glasses
    8 Claret Glasses
    11 [Semanao?] Glasses
    6 glass Custard Cups
    3 glass Sugar & Cream
    2 Cut Glass Dishes
    12 Blue China Custard Cups
    9 Blue Liverpool Custard Cups
    6 blue patty Pans

1 Desert Set Complete
1 Cheese Tray
1 pair Candle Sticks
1 Backgammon Board
Box of Bottles
2 Dishes & Covers
2 Fire Buckets

China Closet
1 Tea Set
1 Set Plated Castors
2 pair Plated Candlesticks
1 pair Plated Cake Basket
1 pair Plated Salt Cellars
5 pair Decanters
3 Red Waiters
4 old Waiters
2 pair glass Salt Cellars

Front Chamber
1 Kidminster Capet
1 Mahogany Bedstead Bed Bolster Pillows Curtains & Counterpain
6 Chairs
Washstand Bowl & Ewer
1 Bureau
1 Fire Set Complete
1 Lolling Chair & Cover
1 Looking Glass
1 Large Green Cloth
1 Marseilles Quilt

Middle Chamber
1 Carpet
1 Mahogany Bedstead Bed Bolster & Pillows Curtains & Counterpain & old Bed
underneath
1 Single Bedstead Bed & Bolster
1 Mahogany Book Case
4 vol. Dictionary Arts & Sciences
Books in Book Case
9 Coarse Towels
7 Table Cloths
21 Daylas [or Day Cas?]
5 Napkins
9 Cotton Sheets
5 Linen Sheets
10 Linen Pillow Cases
4 Cotton Pillow Cases
2 Green & 1 Plaid Cloth
1 piece new Linen 23 yds.
6 Leather bottom Chairs
1 large Chair
1 Rocking Chair
1 Ward Robe

2 Gowns
1 Cloak & 1 new Coat
6 old [Surtoug?] Cloaks & Coats
4 old Hats
2 Military Hats
23 pair Stockings & other Contents of draw
7 Shirts & contents of draw
vests Flannels etc.
Small Clothes Vests etc. in 3d. daw
1 Sword & Pistols
Military Clothes
Contents of uper draw in Ward Robe
Wash Stand bowl & Pitcher
1 Looking Glass
6 Powder horns
4 Guns
1 Shot bag & shot mould
Indian bow & quiver of arrows
Indian gourd Silver Mounted & covered [Boute?]
4 Cams & 2 Rules
1 Umbrella
15 Tumblers
12 Wine Glasses
Knives & forks
1 Copper Plate Warmer
Lot of Blue China
1 plated Fish Knife
Table Brush
2 Blanc Moulds

Kitchen
2 Mahogany Tables
2 painted Tables
4 Chairs
1 Light Stand
Andirons Shovel Tongs Hooks etc.
Boiler
3 pair Flat Irons
3 pair Lamps & Nurse Lamp
1 Looking Glass
5 Dish Covers
1 pair Bluises

Back Kitchen
Butter Tray
3 arm chairs
4 Pewter Dishes
Lot of Tin Ware
Lot of Crockery
4 Brass Skillets
1 Brass Kettle
1 Bell [Mettle?] Kettle

1 Warming pan & Confectionary Kettle
a lot of Wooden Ware etc.
Family Scales, Weights Morter & Pistel
1 Iron Pot No.1
1 Iron Pot No. 2
1 Copper Pot No. 3
1 Copper Fish Kettle No. 8
1 Copper Fish Kettle No. 4
1 Pot Dish Kettle No. 5
1 Frying pan & 2 Stew Pans
1 Coffee Mill & [Vice?]
Spits, Waffle Iron & Coffee Roaster
Sundrees in Basket
3 Grid irons & Wooden Bowl
1 Pan Sheets
Lot of Towels & Table Cloths
1 pair Spurrs

Wood House
Steps & Window Machine
1 Chamber pail & hod
1 Wheel Barrow
3 Wash Tubs
1 Crow Bar
2 Wood Saws Horse & butte
3 Axes

Chaise House & Barn
1 Chaise & harness
1 Sleigh
3 Garden Rakes & Scythe
Saddle and Bridles
Shovels Spade Hoe & Fork
Horse & Hay
Sundress in Barn Chamber not including Hay
Old [Sashes?] Chairs etc. in Chaise House Closet
1 Horse Cart

Cellar
1 Pipe Cider
4 Gross Bottles
1 Bar Pork
15 Pots & Jugs Pickles
Lot of Vegetables
3 Demijohns
1 Barrel Apples
3 Bottles Oil
1 Oil Canister & Oil
Sundry old Casks
2 Bottles Catsup
Small bag Corks 4 groce
34 [lb?] Pork
2 Silver Tea Pots

1 Silver Cream Pot
1 Silver Sugar Bowl
1 Silver pair Sugar Tongs
4 Silver Small Ladles
1 Silver Large Ladle
1 Silver Tankard
3 Silver Cans
2 Silver Poringers
3 Salt Spoons
16 Tea Spoons
10 Table Spoons

APPENDIX SIX

1860 CENSUS WARD ONE, BOSTON

Melinde Lutz Sanborn

The 1860 Census for Ward One, Boston, Massachusetts: Some Special Features and Flaws

The 1860 Federal census for Ward One, Boston, Massachusetts, is an invaluable resource for persons attempting to locate the origins of those who passed through this largely Irish community. However, a sloppy job of transcription casts doubt on the accuracy of its revelations and caution must be exercised in using the various copies of this work.

In 1860 Boston's Ward One spanned part of the area now known as the North End, which includes historic Copp's Hill. A largely Italian neighborhood today, it once embraced hundreds of immigrant Irish families. Ordinarily, such as area would not be expected to yield much in the way of detailed records, given the cultural and economic barriers between the inhabitants and the established record-keeping authorities. It is a special treat, therefore, to discover that the 1860 Ward One enumerator, William B. Tarlton, interpreted the instructions for the "Place of Birth" column to require an exact town when in the United States or a county or province when in a foreign country.

Although documentation of Irish origins can sometimes be discovered through newspaper obituaries or advertisements, gravestone inscriptions, naturalizations, vital records of the immigrant or descendants, and church records, this is usually hit-or-miss research. And for the era preceding 1860, passenger lists are still rare or uninformative and Boston vital records are dramatically incomplete. Therefore, the detailed set of entries in the Ward One Boston census offers a remarkable source of origins for members on its 3,353 resident households. For the hundreds of young Irish women who arrived in Boston as single domestics, this census is often a last-chance opportunity for specific information, since there women characteristically did not naturalize in their own right.

Thanks to Mr. Tarlton's thoroughness, it is possible to make a few characterizations about the Irish population of Ward One in 1860 from the census in a far more specific manner than in any other ward of the city. As Ward One was a small, economically defined area, home to only about 5,000 persons, it cannot be used to represent Boston's Irish population in general. However, it does supply some very valuable information.

The following counties in Ireland were represented (only individuals giving specific counties are included here; 1,021 of the 5,000 respondents were recorded under the general heading "Ireland" and are not included in the percentages given below):

Cork	27.6%
Donegal	15.3%
Galway	8.4%
Sligo	4.5%
Derry	4.2%
Dublin	3.6%
Fermanagh	3.6%
Leitrim	3.1%
Tyrone	3.0%
Kerry	2.2%
Waterford	1.9%
Londonderry	1.9%
Mayo	1.8%
Tipperary	1.6%
Made	1.5%
Limerick	1.5%
Clare	1.38%

Louth, Roscommon, and other counties represented less than 1.3% each.

Again, based on too small and too specific a sample to draw conclusions regarding the Boston Irish population in general, certain intermarriage patterns surfaced in Ward One. While men and women from all Irish counties were more likely to marry persons from the same county, the most popular exogamous pattern was for an Irish man to marry an American woman (a detailed study of this phenomenon would most likely reveal that these American women were first generation children of Irish immigrants). While most of the American women were from Boston, points as distant as China, Maine, and Northport, New York, were represented. Irish men were almost twice as likely to marry American women as Irish women were to marry American men. Yet Irish women in Ward One were almost twice as likely to marry men from foreign countries than their male counterparts. Also, while Irish men married only women from English-speaking countries, Irish women also married French and Prussian men.

Among inter-Irish marriages, men and women from Donegal were most likely to marry out of their county, followed by women and men from Sligo. This finding may be skewed by the fact that clusters of persons from these counties are found in Ward One in unrepresentative numbers on contiguous streets. Other intermarriages were too rare to form a pattern. It is interesting to note that men and women from Donegal chose spouses from Sligo more often than from any other county except their own. Some of these exogamous marriages can be seen as a function of immigration, but the degree to which this is true cannot be measured precisely due to prejudiced reporting of children's birthplaces. One of the few ways to approximately date and place a marriage of an immigrant couple in the census is to observe the place of birth of their children. Unfortunately, there was a strong inclination to claim American birthplaces for all children in a family, even when in actuality the oldest were foreign-born.

The specificity of origins listed in the Ward One census is a gold mine to researchers. However, the 1860 census demonstrates other peculiarities which are not as helpful. It is generally known that the enumerator, after making his rounds, returned to his office and transcribed his notes onto the familiar printed forms which were later bound into the census as we recognize it. In all, three copies were made of the census in the period 1850 to 1870; a county, a state, and a federal copy. Presumably, the rough notes were destroyed.

Little attention has been focused on the question of which of the several copies came first. By and large, it appears that the differences between them have been ignored because these are so slight, and it is the federal copy which is most often used. This is not the case with the 1860 Ward One, Boston census, however.

The state copy of 1860 Ward One is available in handwritten book form at the Massachusetts State Archives. For local researchers this presents a welcome relief from microfilm records, but it has its own problems. The book suffers from numerous erasures and extensive handling. Quite a number of pages are entered in incorrect order, i.e., page 40 follows page 36, 56 follows 52, 60 follows 55, 163 follows 160, 179 follows 176, and 304 follows 300. The federal copy suffers from similar inconsistencies, but on different pages. This poses a serious problem for the researcher who, attempting to retrace the steps of the census-taker using a ward map and city directory, stumbles upon one of these reversals.

There are many reasons for tracing the enumerator's progress through a city. Beyond the obvious time-saving advantage of narrowing down the number of pages to be searched when a family's city address is known, following the enumerator can open the way to a more effective use of city directories. Directories often provide more specific information on an individual or a family than can be found in the census: everything from the date of removal to a new city, place of employment, exact death dates, to the name of a widow's late husband. However, when the city directory lists seventeen Joseph Kellys distinguished only by different addresses, the census can help to identify them. Also, it is often much easier to spot the proper family in the census when one is given names of spouses or children to match or discard. Until 1880, street addresses were not included in the federal census. Thus, one can match the names of persons who appear before and after the family listed in Ward One census with city directory entries until a pattern develops and the proper address is determined. If pages are reversed, the census "neighbors" are out of order and confusion results.

Professor Peter R. Knights'census finding aid (Index to the Manuscript Censuses of Boston [1976], manuscript, Massachusetts State Archives) exposes the damage done by enumerators who moved randomly throughout Ward One. Professor Knights constructed a columnar outline using the family number assigned in the census and the 1860 Boston city directory to trace the order in which the enumerator visited households. This serves as a useful shortcut in searching the unindexed census. Construction of such a finding aid is carefully detailed in Keith R. Schlesinger's "An 'Urban Finding Aid' for the Federal Census" (Prologue, Winter, 1981), 251-262. Further discussion is found in Keith Schlesinger and Peggy Tuck Sinko, "Urban Finding Aid for Manuscript Census Searchers," *National Genealogical Society Quarterly* 69[1981]:171-180.

Page reversals pale in comparison with a second major flaw in the state copy. It would appear that in transcribing, the clerk copied in columns rather than by following each individual's entry horizontally across the page. It becomes painfully obvious, after several startling entries, that the copyist lost track of the columns and omitted or duplicated certain entries, throwing off the remainder of the page until he caught the error. Was little Mary Douglas, at the tender age of one, really a tailoress (family #54)? And Ann M. Montgomery a carpenter (family #55)? Was Joseph P. Murphy (ostensibly the father of James Murphy), really born in Boston about 1802 while James was born in Cork, Ireland, about 1820 (family #200)? This last is an illustration of the most troublesome of the errors – and the most difficult to spot. Rather than supplying an exciting clue to the Murphy's origin in Co. Cork, Ireland, it suggests that the researcher must consider the birthplaces several spaces above and below the entry.

To complicate matters, it is not always clear exactly where the omissions or duplications were first made nor when or how the correction occurred. The clerk never acknowledged the error with inserts or crossed-out lines, but brazenly used dittos to even out each numbered page. On one occasion, the copyist actually appears to have considered turning the last two children on the page into twins to even out the line (family #205).

It was no easy matter for one enumerator to tackle an entire Boston ward. In Ward One this is clearly illustrated in the content of the answers to the birthplace question. Through this column we can see that either William Tarlton became very hurried on the 21st and 23rd of July or that at least two enumerators were used. Large portions of the third quarter of Ward One done on these days shows only "Ireland" as a place of birth. At least three copyists did the transcribing in the ward. Their handwriting styles differ markedly. Two hands span the imprecise "Ireland" responses but both hands recorded county answers in other sections of the ward.

It is encouraging that the federal copy does not appear to make as many errors as the state copy. Although the names and spelling frequently differ, it is clear that the federal copy, in this instance, came first.

Once these flaws are taken into consideration, the 1860 Ward One census proves to be an important source. Small clues to Irish origins, such as the Donegal-Sligo connection and the specific county designations in the 1860 Ward One Boston census are sufficiently rare to deserve significant attention. While nothing can supersede an in-depth study of the history and character of an area like Ward One in assisting the study of origins, the 1860 census for this area can serve as a valuable introduction.

APPENDIX SEVEN

EXAMPLES FROM INSTITUTIONAL RECORDS

The records of the following Massachusetts Institutions are at ARCH and FHL.

In the course of doing research, you may find information in family papers, or in a state or Federal census, that a family member spent some time in or even lived at one of these institutions, or you may find on a death certificate that they died at one of these institutions. Most of the registers and records of case histories that I looked at were indexed either in the front or the back of the volume. Several years ago while transcribing the 1855 and 1865 Massachusetts state censuses, I found a man named Nothing Particular in the Ipswich Insane Asylum in 1855 and at the Tewksbury State Almshouse in 1865. In the Register of weekly admissions and discharges at the almshouse, it is reported that Nothing Particular, who was admitted to the almshouse March 31, 1857, died September 7, 1895 at age seventy-three.

Institutions for the Poor

State Almshouse, Monson
Admission records and case histories, 1854–1882

This example from Great Barrington shows the basic form used by towns throughout Massachusetts to send people to the Monson Almshouse:

> September 13, 1871, The Superintendent of State Almshouse, at Monson, Will please admit the following person from Great Barrington; name, Angeline Garrison, age 46, birthplace Hillsdale in State of New York, Came into State 1868, last time; this is signed by the overseers of the poor of Great Barrington. Additional questions on this form show that Angeline's parents were Henry and Mary (Makeley) Garrison, born in New York; the father died in Austerlitz, New York, and the mother lives in Albany, New York; her grandfather was Jacob Makeley of Hillsdale.

On September 26, 1871, Worcester sent 3-1/2-year old Alexander Benton, born in Rhode Island, son of Alexander Benton, to Monson. On the back of the form is this:

> This child was brought to Worcester by His Father who states that the mother is dead; he was born in one of the Southern States and served in the Rebel Army during the war, and is now in Fitchburg Jail under sentence of one Year for Assault with intent to murder; he married an Irish woman in Worcester, and afterwards informed her he had another wife in Rhode Island, and all he wanted for her was to take care of the child - which she now refuses to do.

> Mary Godfrey, of Sprague St., W. Springfield. Born Sept. 10, 1877 in Springfield. Fa. John [dead], Mo. Ellen. This girl's father is dead and her mother in jail, Springfield, for drunkenness. She has been arrested several times for this offence. There are two other children, John about 14 years old, is in the Hampden County Truant school, Charles, about 15 years old is at work for the M.U.Tel. Co. in Springfield and is self supporting. After commitment of the mother, this girl had no home. She is bright and attractive and should be placed out.

> John J. Connors. Father Michael Connors died in 1878. Mother Betsey died in 1879, soon after adopted by Patrick & Rose Keegan. Has had a good home, but disposed to take things not his own. On Friday stole a watch chain, rings & ball from a store on E. Main St., Fall River.

> Harry Sheldon of Curtisville, Stockbridge. Born Mch. 1880 in Chatham, N.Y. Fa. Horatio N. - Mo. Maria (dead). This boy with his older brother was before the Court at Lee last Jan. 9 as neglected children, but father said he was going to remove to N.Y. Instead he moved to Stockbridge. He keeps house himself & works out on a farm and locks the children out of doors day times. They are little thieves. Have been implicated before. Sat. Oct. 5th they broke into the house of a Mr. Clapper and stole a number of small articles and did quite an amount of mischief. The father is an old man and is said to have been in jail several times. He has very little control over the boys.

> John C. Rochford, born Feb. 23, 1882, Alice J. Rochford, born Feb. 24, 1884, and Mary E. Rochford, born Aug. 23, 1885, all born in Springfield. Fa. Geo. J., Mo. Mary [dead]. Family have been aided a good deal. About a year ago the father got drunk and smashed the furniture and turned his wife out of doors, though since there has been but little trouble. The mother died Dec. 7th and the children were found last Wednesday ragged and dirty at the home of their grandmother who says she can find places for them but could not show that she had found any suitable persons willing to take them.

The registers of births contain the births of many illegitimate children, but in most cases the father's name as well as the mother's name are given. For example: William Sullivan, born October 1, 1866, son of Julia Sullivan and William O'Brien; and John Barry, born March 3, 1860, son of Margaret Barry and Patrick McCarty.

The registers of deaths contain the name of the deceased, age, death date, cause of death, parents' names, sex, and birthplace. For example, Elizabeth O'Brien, age two, died Oct 15, 1874, of scrofula, daughter of Martin and Maria O'Brien, female, born Oxford; and Oren Johnson, age eight, died March 31, 1875, of pneumonia, son of John H. and Francena Johnson, male, born Richmond, New Hampshire.

State Primary School at Monson
Case histories 1864–1895
Boarding out register 1883–1892
Placement register 1874–1890
School records 1854–1895

The admission forms to the State Primary School at Monson are on stationery from the "State Board of Lunacy and Charity, Department of In-Door Poor." The form begins as follows:

> "To the Superintendent State Primary School, Dear Sir: Please receive and provide for Mary Godfrey, committed to the custody of the Board by Police Court at Springfield, on the third day of September 1882, for the offence of Neglected."

At the bottom are explanations of how the child came to be sent to the State school, such as this:

> Irene T. Chapman, of Main St., Natick. Born April 1, 1877 in Cochituate. Father Charles K. Mother, Margaret. The parents of Irene are dead. Father died 1885, Mother 1884. Since their deaths she has been living most of the time with her maternal grandmother, Mrs. Catherine Martin, 299 North St., Boston. Mrs. Martin keeps a house of ill-fame and dance hall at that place. On Sept. 15th Irene ran away from there and went to her paternal grandmother, Mrs. Lucy Chapman in Natick where she has since resided. Irene has a very bad temper and when asked to do anything replies with vile and abusive language. Has thrown knives and dishes at her grandmother and torn up her bed clothes. Mrs. Chapman being an old lady was in constant fear and for that reason had her complained of.

The school made indenture agreements that placed many children with families throughout New England; sample indentures show placements in Massachusetts as well as Providence, Rhode Island; Hillsborough, New Hampshire; East Windsor, Connecticut; and a rare placement in Woodsdale, Butler County, Ohio. The boys were in most cases to learn agriculture or farming and the girls, housekeeping. At the end of their indenture, when the boys were twenty-one and the girls were eighteen, they were to be given a certain sum of money, usually $50 but sometimes as high as $100, and two suits of clothing, one for the Sabbath and one for working days, and sometimes to provide them with a Bible.

The records of the hospital at the State Primary School contain the name of the patient, age, birthplace, whether single or married, occupation, previous health, habits, color, date of admission, disease, result (whether they got well or died), and remarks. For example, Catherine O'Donnell, age $3^{1/2}$ months, born Boston, white, admitted July 25, diarrhea, died July 28, mother had syphilis.

State Almshouse, Tewksbury
Children's records, 1855–1869
Inmate case histories, 1860–1896
Weekly returns of admission and discharge, 1894–1918

> Simeon Ford, colored, 30, from Charlestown February 13, 1868, born NY, single, laborer, came to MA from NY 2 years ago via O.C.&N.R.R., in state prison for horse stealing since, no relations in MA, mother Mrs. Frances Bird in NY, in no other institutions, well.

> Frank Silva, 5, from Boston February 13, 1868, born Boston, mother arrested, father off, sent from Little Wanderers Home.

> Mary Curtis, 18, from Boston August 2, 1867, born Deerfield, single, domestic, lived in Deerfield most of life, mother died when she was young, father Charles died 6 years last September in Deerfield, never owned property, don't know where born always lived in Deerfield, no relatives living, never in institution before, father of child Frank Steele, saw him last in Deerfield 8 months ago, he a hard drinker and gambler, left there now, sick soon, Grandfather Gibben - farmer, mother Lucinda Smith of South Hadley.

> Honora Sullivan, 35, from Boston August 3, 1867, born Ireland, married husband John, off 2 weeks, landed NY per "Wm. Tapicott," direct to Boston, 1 year to South Natick, then to South Natick 5 years, then to Boston since, husband never in service, no relatives, never in institution before, well, couldn't take care of family. [With her were] Margaret Sullivan, 10, born South Natick; Daniel, 8, born South Natick; Timothy, 7, born Boston; Michael, 15, born London, England; and Jeremiah, 12, born South Natick.

The children in the State Almshouse were often placed with families throughout Massachusetts and the follow-up visits until they were of age (eighteen for girls and twenty-one for boys) can provide a glimpse of their lives. Margaret Donovan was admitted from Boxford August 9, 1860, at age ten, she had been born in Lowell. She was taken by William Stevens, Jr., of Marblehead in September 1860. A visit to Stevens on November 20, 1867, found that she had stayed with him for four years when he placed her with his father William Stevens, Sr., where she had been for about a year. She was reported to be " 'below par' in intellect, not capable of taking care of herself, untruthful & careless about her person, rather given to lewdness." On November 6, 1868, Margaret was returned to the Almshouse on account of mental disability. In January 1869 she was taken on trial by Henry E. Worcester of Tewksbury and a visit on March 9, 1869, found "Margaret happy & contented, likes her place well."

These records also contain the extraodinary story of George G. Leaverns, born in England and came to Massachusetts in 1844, who was admitted from Lowell on January 10, 1856. He was taken by Mrs. Nathaniel Lowe of Tewksbury June 24, 1856.

> [emphasis in original] A remarkable case of self education & perseverance under difficulties. George was with the Lowes about 4 years - previous to his going there, while at the almshouse, had the fingers of his left hand cut off in a hay cutter; in the army, at battle of Fredericksburg, was shot in the right arm which was amputated at the shoulder; returned to Maine, after leaving hospital, fitted himself for College; went to college, & is now holding high position as a teacher at Rochester N.Y. Universal....It appears that his family had oringinally occupied a good position in society, but the father died; hard times came upon them, the mother & boy had to go to the Almshouse; the mother died there, & on her death bed got a pledge from the boy that when out of the institution, he would so act all thru life so to gain an honorable name; well has George kept his pledge.

Not all the stories of these children turn out so well. Timothy Keenan was placed with William Babb of North Barrington, New Hampshire, in 1864. When representatives of the almshouse visited in August 1868, they were told that Timothy had been with Babb only three or four months when he was returned to Dr. McDaniel, who placed him with George Ham of Stafford, New Hampshire. In September the representative "on my way to Stafford to see Mr. Ham, met a gentleman...who told me that the boy was not there; had left about 2 years before & that it was a hard place for a child....Mr. Hamm is represented as being not a good master to send children to; he works them too hard & does not school them as he ought."

State Industrial School for Girls
Case histories 1856–1908

Lyman School for Boys or State Reform School, Westborough
Commitment registers 1848–1891

Medical Institutions

Boston Insane Hospital or Lunatic Hospital

Hospital Cottages for Children
Medical records, 1882–1918

Massachusetts State Hospital, Boston
Institutional registers, 1855–1907

Massachusetts School for Idiotic and Feeble-minded Youth
Medical Records, 1864–1909

Massachusetts Commission on Mental Diseases
Registers of patients in private hospitals, 1843–1917

In the register that covers from 1884 to 1914 there are listed forty-two private asylums or doctors licensed to take mental patients. The register is organized by the various asylums or doctors such as the private asylum at Norwood run by Dr. Eben C. Norton, or Pine Terrace at Baldwinville run by Dr. W.F. Robie. Information contained includes the name of the patient, age, sex, civil condition, birthplace, residence, committed by, committed from, committed on, discharged on, removed by, and remarks. The residences of the patients are from all over New England and places even further away such as Baltimore, Maryland; and Fargo, North Dakota.

Massachusetts State Board of Insanity
Boarding out Registers, 1885–1904

Military Records of Hospital Care, Rainsford Island, Boston, 1854–1866

Massachusetts State Hospital, Danvers
Medical records, 1878–1917

The personal and medical histories of the patients include the basic information as well as comments over time. For example: Mary McGillicuddy, residence Somerville, born Medford, committed by Justice of the Police Court, Middlesex County, age 22, occupation Domestic, single, age of first attack 21; her mother was Mrs. Stephen Lynch, 440 No. Ave., Cambridge; her brother was John McGillicuddy, 60 Sydney St., Cambridgeport. She was admitted on Oct. 13, 1879, for "Overwork with great worry." The doctor on her admittance noted "she is very quiet & undemonstrative before strangers & only after seeing her several times could be satisfied she would be benefited by treatment in a hospital." Notes continued to be made: Aug. 1883, "Never speaks to anyone."; Jan. 1887, "has progressed with remarkable monotony"; June 1890, "Remains just the same"; June 1892, "Neat in appearance. Industrious"; Oct. 1895, "Works steadily on the ward every day"; and Aug. 1897, "Still industrious, but more sociable than at last note."

Massachusetts State Hospital, Grafton
Inpatient case files 1877-1919

Massachusetts State Hospital, Foxborough
Institutional registers, 1893–1918

Massachusetts State Hospital, Medfield
Institutional registers, 1896–1906

Hospital for Epileptics, Monson
Medical records, 1898–1918

In addition to the almshouse, Monson also had a Hospital for Epileptics. The records contain the name of the patient, whether sane or insane, age, sex, civil condition, birthplace, residence, occupation, how committed, committed from, date of commission, how supported (by state, town, or private), date of discharge, how removed, and remarks. For example, George Mullin, insane, age 13, male, single, born Boston, residence Holyoke, no occupation, admitted from Northampton Hospital February 25, 1902, supported by the town, died October 30, 1905, from exhaustion from epilepsy.

Massachusetts State Hospital, Northampton
Institutional registers, 1858–1907

State Sanatorium, Rutland
Patients' register, 1898–1918

The patient's registers are quite informative, containing the date of admission, name and address of patient, sex, age, married or single, religion, occupation, place of business, dependents, trial, date of discharge, who is paying for the hospital, family physician, friends, place and date of birth, and mother's and father's names and places of birth. Other registers also included length of stay in days and result. On January 30, 1900, Chas. T. Crook of Attleboro was admitted; he was male, age sixteen, single, protestant, worked in a jewelry shop, dependent was his father, send bill to father, physician was Dr. A.A. Amsden of Attleboro, friends were his father A.W. Crook of Attleboro and his mother, S.W. Crook, of Plainville; he was discharged on May 5, 1900, after a stay of ninety-six days but was not improved, in fact worse. On May 1, 1905, Frederick E. Marsh of 380 Court St., Ware was admitted; he was male, age forty-eight, married, protestant, a self-employed silver plater, had a wife and four children as dependants; he was discharged August 31, 1905; he was paying for his stay himself; his physician was Dr. Pearson of Ware; his friends were his wife Mrs. Frederick Marsh, Mr. E.N. Lyman of Ware; he was born at Ware on September 18, 1856, to Wm. C. Marsh, born Hardwick, and Delia B. [Comsear?], born Ware

Massachusetts State Hospital, Taunton
Institutional registers, 1854–1907

Tewksbury Asylum for Chronic Insane
Registers 1866 to 1907

The registers include the patient's name, age, sex, civil condition (single or married), birthplace, residence, transferred from (usually from the almshouse), date of transfer, how supported by state or town, date of discharge, how discharged (usually by death), and remarks. Of the first thirty-five patients admitted when the Asylum opened on October 1, 1866, thirteen were males and twenty-two were females; they ranged in age from fourteen to fifty-five (two had no age recorded); nineteen were born in Ireland, one in England, two in France, one in Scotland, two in Charlestown, one in Lynn, one in Cape Breton, two in Boston, and two in Lowell (four had no birthplace recorded); thirty died while at the Asylum, causes listed for six of them were cerebral hemorrhage, peritonitis, arterioscelerosis, chronic diarrhea, and heart disease, three of them lived into the twentieth century including Bridget Callahan, who died June 7, 1918; and one was transferred to the Worcester Asylum.

Perkins Institution and Massachusetts Asylum for the Blind, Watertown
Medical records, 1864–1875

The Registers of the Perkins Institution and Massachusetts Asylum for the Blind contain the name of the patient, age, birthplace, residence, when admitted, by whom supported, in school or workshop, when left, whether discharged or died, and remarks. For example: Cornelius McCauley, age eight, born Cambridgeport, residence Massachusetts, in school, discharged April 6, 1865, sent to Idiot School; and Isabella S. Batchelder, age thirteen, born Williamsburg, New York, residence Massachusetts, in school, discharged Oct. 1, 1865.

Massachusetts State Hospital, Westborough
Inpatient commitment and institutional registers, 1886–1918

Worcester Insane Hospital or Lunatic Hospital
In Worcester were the Worcester Lunatic Hospital and the Worcester Insane Hospital. The registers for the Lunatic Hospital contain name of the patient, age, sex, civil condition, birthplace, residence, occupation, how committed, committed from, date of commitment, how supported (state, town, private), date of discharge, how removed, and remarks. For example, Minnie Anderson, age thirty-three, female, married, born Norway, residence Boston, occupation housework, committed by the Probate Court in Boston on January 2, 1902, discharged July 9, 1902, improved.

The records contain the name of the patient, age, sex, civil condition, birthplace, residence, occupation, admitting information, how supported, dismissal information. For example, Apolus Howard, age eighty-three, male, white, born Royalston, residence Worcester, no occupation, was admitted by the District Court at Worcester on July 27, 1907, supported by the state, died July 30, 1907 from multiple injuries from falling from a window; Maud L. Smith, age sixty-five, female, married, born Maine, residence Cambridge, no occupation, admitted by the District Court at Cambridge on October 22, 1905, supported by the state, discharged on November 1, 1906, to the care of her family; and Minnie Dorsey, colored, age thirty-four, female, single, born Massachusetts, residence Boston, occupation domestic, admitted by the Probate Court at Boston on October 10, 1905, supported by the state, discharged May 5, 1911 and transferred to the Worcester Asylum.

Correctional Institutions

Suffolk County Sheriff's Records, 1799–1916
Debtor Calendars and Criminal Calenders

Castle Island Commitment Registers, 1785–1798

The registers have columns for Names, Term of Time [date of admittance], By which Court, Which County, Term of Time, Liberated, Escaped, and Died. For example: Robert Hazzard was admitted on Oct. 10, 1790, by the General Session Court of Hampshire County, for two years, and liberated Oct. 10, 1792. James Digman, William English, Samuel Morse, John Ferrin, and Seth Johnson all serving various sentences, escaped on Aug. 2, 1793.

Lyman School for Boys
Daily registers, 1848–1901

Massachusetts State Nautical School
Case histories and commitment register of boys, 1856–1870
Case histories of boys for the School Ship George M. Bernard, 1864–1872

For each boy there is a registered page, the following kind of information is given:

> Frederic A. Mitchell was committed Feb. 6, 1865, by the Probate Court of Suffolk County for Larceny. His residence was 107 Broadway, So. Boston; his hair was brown, eyes dark, and complexion light; he was 5' 5½" in height and weighed 115 pounds. He was born in Charlestown, Nov. 24, 1849, son of John A. Mitchell (b. New Hampshire) and Caroline Mitchell (born Haverhill, NH). His father died 3 years ago and he has one brother and one sister. He has not drunk "ardent spirits," but has used tobacco. He has worked at Algers as a moulder. His companions are Asa Christopher and Frank Bradley. He has attended school three months in succession; left school 1 year ago; has attended church and sabbath school; and had not been arrested before. On June 7, 1860, he was transferred to the school ship; on Aug. 13, 1866, was transferred to the G.M.

Bernard; and on Sept. 14, 1866, shipped out under Capt. Crosby for the East Indies.

George Franklin Smith was committed July 1, 1865, by the Superior Court Bristol County for breaking and entering to steal. His residence was on [Nels?] Table road, New Bedford; his hair was brown, eyes black, complexion light; he was 4' 10¾" in height and weighed 90 pounds; he has a small scar on his right knee from whipping. He was born in Maine, July 17, 1850, son of Samuel Smith (b. Maine) and Mary Ann Soules (born Westford MA). His father and mother separated 3 years ago, his father is in the army, and he has 4 brothers and 4 sisters. He has not drunk ardent spirits, but has used tobacco. He has worked in a bake shop. His companions are Edward Bessee, John Riley, and William Upham. He has attended school three months in succession; left school 2 years ago; has probably attended church and sabbath school; and was once arrested for Larceny and served 6 months in the House of Correction. On June 7, 1866, he was transferred to the school ship, and on Sept. 30, 1866, shipped in the bark Sappho to go whaling.

Massachusetts Reformatory for Women, Framingham
Register of children admitted 1874–1901
Abstracts of inmate registers 1877–1926
Case notebooks 1877–1937
Registers of births 1877–1905
Register of children 1878–1933

The inmate registers have entries such this:

Sophia Jaknbasz Morrissey was admitted Aug. 7, 1934, by the District Court in Springfield for lewd, wanton, and lascivious person in speech and behaviour. She was 27, born Holyoke, residence 2462 Main St., Springfield, 5' 6" in height, 199 pounds, hair brown, complexion dark, eyes blue, build large, appendix scar. Her father was Thomas Jaknbasz, 121 Lyman St., Holyoke; mother Mary Domenik, dead; husband James Morrissey, 2462 Main St., Springfield.

The registers of births have entries such as these:

Mary Agnes Kendall, born Sept. 9, 1880 Ref. Prison Sherborn, color white, female legitimate; father John Kendall, residence Boston, occupation painting, b. Boston; mother Mary Kendall, maiden name Mary Smith, residence Boston, b. England.

Clyde Baldwin, born Dec. 23, 1899; father Joseph Marey, residence Keene NH, shoemaker; mother Emma Baldwin, residence Keene NH.

Helen Kimball, b. Jan. 14, 1900; father Edward Dorvick, residence Waltham, occupation Bicycle Factory; mother Alice Kimball, residence Waltham, b. Lancaster PA.

Charlestown State Prison
Indexes 1805–1930
Entries of convicts 1805–1824
Commitment registers 1818–1930
Warden's memorandum of prisoners 1858–1902
Recommitment register 1805–1831

The heading in the recommitment register is "Names &c. of Convicts who have been committed to the State Prison three times." The columns are Name, Age, Crime, Where born, When committed, Sentence Solitary or Labor, and Remarks. For example: Seth Bailey was committed three times at ages twenty-five, twenty-seven, and twenty-nine for Thieving; he was born in Natick MA; was committed on Nov. 2, 1813, May 5, 1815, and Oct. 12, 1816; he was sentenced to fifteen days solitary and two years labor, five days solitary and one year labor, and five days solitary and two years labor; was discharged in 1818.

Concord Reformatory
Case histories, 1884–1934

For each inmate there is a register page that gives this kind of information:

George E. Dodge was received Sept. 22, 1890, by the E. Midd. First District Court, for False Pretenses and was sentenced to 5 years so his sentence would expire on Sept. 22, 1895. He is temperate, attended common school, occupation hotel hand, and has no property. He was born Oct. 14, 1850 in Massachusetts. His residence at time of arrest was Boston. His mental condition and capacity were good and his moral perceptions were good. He was Protestant and married. He was 5' 5¼" in height, weighed 115 pounds, hair dark brown, eyes black, features thin, complexion dark, beard dark brown, build slim, nose ordinary, ears ordinary, hands ordinary, hat size 6 $^{7/8}$, shoe size 6, teeth good; he had a high forehead and a small wart on right arm just above the elbow. His father was William, born Beverly, present residence Salem; his mother was Lyda Ann, born Salem, died 1881. His wife's name is Kate E., born Cape Briton [sic.], present residence Boston.

The complaint against him: Falsely representing to one Marietta F. Richards of Malden that he had no means of obtaining money to reach his family in Cleveland, and presenting a paper signed Willis P. Odell alleging that he, Dodge, was an earnest christian and a member of the Methodist church in Malden. Whereas: The said Dodge's family was not in Cleveland and that said Odel did not sign any paper alleging that he the said Dodge was an earnest christian and belonged to the Methodist church in Malden.

Report from Office of Commissioners: Has a wife at #40 Dennis St., Boston Highlands; claims to be an upholsterer by trade. Has been married three years and his wife says that he always used her kindly. Ten years ago, Dodge was a member of the Tremont Temple Baptist Church. At this time he acted as clerk for the Rev. Dr. Ellis. He was caught circulating a begging petition in Cambridge at that time by one of the congregation. He soon had to leave that society. When arrested, Dodge had notes in his pocket "showing that he had been shortly before elected President of some religious society."

INDEX

Ackley, Mary, 24

Ackley, Samuel, 24

Ackley, Sarah, 24

"Children of John **Adams** (1661–1702) of Braintree and Boston, Maltster, The" (Lesure), 83

"Nathaniel **Adams** of Weymouth and Boston, Mass." (Wead), 83

Adams, Samuel, 41, 52

admission records (church), 9

adoptions, 24

"Hepzibah **Alden's** Silver Box, The Scandal of Ann Sargent Gage and Some Descendants of Nathaniel (John) Alden" (Lainhart and Williams), 83

"Mixed Up Marys and Elizabeths in the Family of John **Alden**" (Lainhart), 83

"Probable Wife of John (John) **Alden,** The" (Lainhart), 83

Alger, Arthur M., 87

Allair, Mary, 39

Allcock, Elizabeth, 21

Allen, Cameron, 89

Allen, John, 21

Allerton, Isaac, 115

almshouses, 28; *see also* under name of specific institution

American Antiquarian Society: holds Farber Gravestone Collection, 16

American Diaries in Manuscript, 1580–1954 (Matthews), 51

American Diaries Written Prior to 1861 (Matthews), 51

American Jewish Historical Society Library, 13, 91

Amory, Rebecca, 21

Amsden, Dr. A.A., 137

Ancient and Honorable Artillery Company of Massachusetts, 74, 91; roll of members, 73

Anderson, Minnie, 138

Anderson, Robert Charles, 2, 36, 85, 87, 88

"Applications and Admissions to the Homes for Aged Colored Women in Boston, 1860–1887" (Shoenfeld), 29

Applications for Seamen's Certificate of American Citizenship: held at National Archives and Records Administration, 46

apprentices, 23

Archives of the (Catholic) Archdiocese of Boston, 10, 12, 91; records for baptisms, marriages, deaths, or burials, 12; holds records of the Home for Destitute Catholic Children, 12; holds records of Catholic orphanages, 12

Arlington Street Church (Federal Street Church), 8, 10

Ashton Alfred J., 60

Babb, William, 135

Babcock, Elizabeth, 30

"William **Badlam**, Ship Master of Boston and Weymouth and Some of His Descendants" (Cook), 83

Bailey, Seth, 141

Baker Library, Harvard University: collection of business papers, 51

Baldwin, Clyde, 140

Baldwin, Emma, 140

Baldwin Place Church, 8

Baltzell, E. Digby, 77

Baptists in Massachusetts (Brush), 13

Barber, Peter, 117

Barclay, Mrs. John E., 83, 84, 85, 86, 89, 90

Barclay, Rachel E., 83, 85, 88

"**Barlow, Coombs,** and **Warren** of Boston" (Barclay and Barclay), 83

Barnes, Mrs. W. Carroll, 90

Barrel, Abiah, 39

Barrell, John, 39

Barry, John, 132

Barry, Margaret, 132

Bartlett, Joseph Gardner, 90

Bartley, Scott Andrew, 84

Bastian, David, 24

Bastian, Olive, 24

Batchelder, Isabella S., 138

"New Royal Descent for Christopher **Batt,** A" (Fradd), 83

Bayer, Jacob, 68

Beacon Hill: Its Ancient Pastures and Early Mansions (Chamberlain), 77

"**Beadon–Bedon** Family" (Holman), 83

Beard, George, 39

Belknap, Henry Wycoff, 86

Bell, Thomas, 115

"Thomas **Bell,** Boston Executioner, and his Son Thomas Bell of Stonington, Connecticut" (Harris), 84

Benton, Alexander, 132

Benton, Josiah Henry, 38

Bernard, G.M., 139–40

Bessee, Edward, 140

"George **Bethune** of Craigfurdies, Scotland, and Boston, Mass." (Noyes), 84

Bill, Anna, 39

Bird, Frances, 134

birth records, 4, 132; 17th and 18th century included in Record Commissioner Reports, 3; microfilm copies at New England Historic Genealogical Society, Boston Public Library and Family History Libraries of the Church of Jesus Christ of Latter Day Saints, 4

Bittle, Thomas, 20

Black Boston: African American Life and Culture in Urban America, 1750–1860 (Levesque), 79

Black Bostonians, Family Life and Community Struggle in the Antebellum North (Horton and Horton), 78

"Abigail Arnold, Wife of Solomon **Blake** of Dorchester, Mass." (Barclay), 84

"John **Blanchard** of Boston, Mass. and Some of His Descendants" (Hartman), 84

Blatt, Warren, 17, 70, 77

"Descendants of John **Blower** of Boston" (Pitman), 84

Bodge, George M., 43

BOSTON 1700–1980, The Evolution of Urban Politics (Formisano and Burns), 77

Boston and Some Noted Emigres: A Collection of Facts and Incidents with Appropriate Illustrations Relating to Some Well-Known Citizens of France who Found Homes in Boston and New England . . ., 75

Boston Asylum: records of, 24

Boston Athenaeum, 91

Boston Beginnings 1630–1699 (Holbrook), 78

"Boston Churches and Ministers" (Hayward), 9

Boston City Archives, 4, 92; and church records, 8; tax valuation records, 50; census holdings, 55, 56; and voter lists, 59; indexes of naturalized voters, 59; holds records of teachers, 63; records of permits for demolished buildings, 73

Boston City Census, 1820, 55–57; *see also* censuses

Boston England and Boston New England, 75

Boston Female Asylum, 26; registers of, 26

Boston French, The (Forbes), 71

Boston Insane Hospital (Lunatic Hospital): records of, 28

Boston Lunatic Hospital: *see* Boston Insane Hospital

Boston Overseers of the Poor: records, 24

Boston Parks Department: and cemetery records, 15

Boston Pilot: runs advertisements for missing relatives, 70

Boston Police Department Records Center and Archives, 92; holds photographs, Brinks Robbery file, diaries, Police Department Annual Reports, 73

Boston Public Library, 15, 19–21, 92; birth records, 4; Admissions to the Town of Boston, 20; records of the Overseers of the Poor, 24; records of the Court of Common Pleas, 39; tax records, 49, 50; photographic collection, 73

Boston Record Commissioners Report, 113–17; minutes of town meetings, 19, 113; selectmen's meeting records, 19, 113; tax lists, 49, 113; Aspinwall Notarial Records, 113

Boston Record Commissioners Reports: contents, 19–21; Admissions to the Town of Boston, 20, 22; tax lists, 49; *see also* Boston Record Commissioners Report

Boston Registry Archives, 92; birth, marriage and death records, 4

Boston Sea Fencibles' Signal Roll, 46–47

Boston Taxpayers in 1821 (Rohrbach), 49

Boston Town Records: in Boston Records Commissioners Reports, 20

Boston University School of Theology Library (Methodist), 13, 92

Boston's Growth. A Bird's Eye View of Boston's Increase in Territory and Population From It's Beginning to the Present, 75

Boston's Immigrants 1840–1925 (Price and Sammarco), 2, 69, 80

Boston's Story in Inscriptions: Being Reproductions of the Markings That Are or Have Been on Historic Sites, 76

Bostonian Society: photographic collection, 73; library, 92

Bostonian Society Publications, The: tax records, 49

Boston—One Hundred Years a City. A Collection of Views Made from Rare Prints and Old Photographs Showing the Changes Which Have Occurred in Boston During One Hundred Years of Its Existence as a City, 1822–1922, 75

"Zacheus **Bosworth**, of Boston, Husbandman" (Montgomery), 84

"Some Additions to Torrey's Marriages: Trerise, Lynde, **Bourne**" (Fiske), 84

Bowditch, Nathaniel Ingersoll, 19

Boyle, Mrs. William, 28

"Boyle's Occurances," 51

Boylston, Peter, 40

"Peter **Brackett** of Braintree and Boston, With Notes on His Daughter, Sarah (Brackett) (Shaw) (Benjamin) Jimmerson" (Harris), 84

Bradford, Capt. John, 24

Bradford, Eliphalet, 38

Bradford, James, 38

Bradford, William, 38

Bradford, Zadok, 38

"Non-*Mayflower* **Bradfords** of New England: Descendants of Robert Bradford of Boston" (Lainhart and Bartley), 84

Bradley, Frank, 139

Brand, John, 40

Brandon, John C., 87

Brattle Street Church: *see* Fourth Church

Brayton, John Anderson, 90

Brice, John, 22

"Family of Henry **Bridgman** of Thelnetham Co. Suffolk, England, and Boston, Mass., The" (Coddington), 84

Bridgman, Thomas, 15

Brinks Robbery Case File: *see* Boston Police Department Records Center and Archives

"William and Mary **Briggs** of Boston and the Connecticut Valley with Notes on Their Sons-in-Law John Harris and Wolston Brockway" (Harris), 84

Bromfield Street Church, 8

Brookens, Jns, 20

"**Brough** Family of Marshfield and Boston, The" (Barclay), 84

Brown, Abigail, 29

Brush, John Woolman, 13

"Old Boston Families: The **Bryant** Family" (Chamberlain), 84

Bulfinch's Boston, 1787–1817 (Kirker), 2, 78

Bumstead, Jeremiah: diaries of, 51

Bunker Hill Cemetery, 16

Burke, Michael, 60

Burkett, Brigitte, 21

Burns, Constance K., 77

Butledge, G.E., 30

"James **Butler**, Vintner, of Boston: A Critique of 'Butleriana'" (Montgomery), 84

"John Harding of Boreham, Essex [**Buttolph**]" (McCracken), 84

"Old Boston Families: The **Byles** Family" (Eaton), 84

Cain, Susannah, 39

"Ancestry of Robert **Calef** of Boston" (Rasmussen), 84

Caley, Daniel, 39

"Descendants of Ellis **Callender** of Boston" (Woodworth-Barnes), 84

Callender, George, 39

Callender, Johanna, 39

Cambridge Catholic Cemetery, 16, 17

Cappuccia, Angelo, 44

Card, Lucy G.M., 63

Carney, James, 28

Carney, John B., 85

"Bigamy in Boston: The Case of Matthew **Cary** and Mary Sylvester" (Simons), 85

Casaburi, Victor F.A., 77

Casey, James P., 44

Casno, Margaret, 35

Castle Island Commitment Registers, 1785–1798, 139

Caswell, Elijah, 52

Cathedral of the Holy Cross, 12

Catholic churches, 10–12

Cazneau (Cusenoe) (Casno), Paix, 35

"Descendants of Paix **Cazneau**" (Lainhart), 85

cemeteries, 15–17; Catholic, 16

censuses: 1800 Federal for Boston, 55; 1860 Federal Census, Ward One, 55, 125–29; 1820 Boston (city), 55–56; William Tarlton enumerator in 1860, 125, 126; intermarriage patterns in 1860, 126, 127; three copies of 1860, 127, 128, 129

Central Cemetery, 15

Century of Town Life: A History of Charlestown, Massachusetts, 1775–1887, A (Hunnewell), 81

Chaffin, Eliza, 20

Chamberlain, Allen, 77

Chamberlain, George Walter, 84

Chamberlain, Mellen, 81

Champney, William Ingersoll, 44

Chapin, Aaron, 50

Chapman, Charles K., 133

Chapman, Irene T., 133

Chapman, Lucy, 133

Chapman, Margaret, 133

Charles Street Baptist Church, 8

Charlestown Catholic Cemetery, 16, 17

Charlestown Land Records, 1638–1802, 81

Charlestown State Prison: records of, 141

Cheever, Eleanor, 51

Child, Katherine, 39

Child, Thomas, 39

Christ Church, 8

Christopher, Asa, 139

Chronicle of Boston Jewry from the Colonial Settlement to 1900, A (Ehrenfried), 14

church records: Protestant, 7–10; Catholic, 10–12

Churches of Christ of the Congregational Way in New England, The (Taylor), 13

Citizen Seamen's Identification Cards: records of, 46

city directories, 41–42, 128

City of Boston: census, 55; *see also* censuses

civil marriage records, 9

Civil War, 44, 46

Clap, Josiah, 24

Clapper, Mr., 132

Clark, Joseph S., 13

"Widow Mary Ring, of Plymouth, Mass., and Her Children [**Clark**]" (Coddington), 85

Clark, William H., 82

Clarke, Mrs. R.P., 29

Cleary, John, 70

Cleary, Michael, 70

Cleary, Patrick, 70

Cleary, Thomas, 70

Cleary, William, 70

Cobb, David, 78

Cochran, Lucretia, 26

Coddington, John Insley, 84, 85, 87, 88, 90

Codman, Mrs., 27

"Parentage of John **Cole** of Boston, Mass., and Rhode Island" (Holman), 85

Coleman, Hiram H., 61

Coleman, Marie E., 61

Colket, Meredith, 88

"Will of Richard **Collacott** of Boston, Mass., The" (Coddington), 85

"Collection of the Massachusetts Archives Civil War Records," 44

Colletta, John Philip, 71

Colonial Clergy of New England (Weis), 9

Colonial History of East Boston (Casaburi), 77

Colonial Society of Massachusetts: and legal records, 37

Commonwealth of Massachusetts, Military Division—History Research and Museum: military records from 1776–1940, 44, 92

"Complete List of the Ministers of Boston of all Denominations, from 1630 to 1842, A," 9

Compton, John, 115

Comsear, Delia B: *see* Ware, Delia B.

Concord Reformatory: records of, 141

"Parentage and English Progenitors of Nathaniel **Coney** of Boston, Mass." (Hills), 85

Congregation Ohabei Shalom (Jewish): cemetery, 17

Congregational Library and Archives, 12, 92

Connors, Betsey, 132

Connors, John J., 132

Connors, Michael, 132

Cook, Wendel B., 83

Coombs: *see* **Barlow**

Cooper, William, 114

Copley Square: A Brief Description of Its History Including a Short Sketch of the Famous Artist for Whom the Square was Named—With Illustrations of Interesting Buildings, Portraits by Copley and Early Views, 77

Copp's Hill Cemetery, 15

Cott, Nancy F., 95

Cotter, Daniel, 59

Cotter, James F., 59

Couet, A.E., 87

Coulter, Patrick, 70

Court of Admiralty: records of, 38

Courts of Assistance: divorce records in, 94

Courts of Common Plea: records of, 39

Courts of General Session: records of, 39

"Court Files Suffolk Births, Marriages, and Deaths Jan 1637/8 to Aug 1774": included in records of Superior Court of Judicature, 4

"Court Files Suffolk": divorce records, 95

courts: records of, 4, 37–40, 95; *see also* various depositories

Cowells, Edward, 22

Cox, Mr. and Mrs., 26

Crook, A.W., 137

Crook, Charles T., 137

Crook, S.W., 137

Crooked and Narrow Streets of Boston, The (Thwing), 32, 80

Crookes, Edward, 23

Crosby, John, 41

Crossthwayte: *see* **Danson**

Cullen, James Bernard, 70

Cumberford, Edward, 39

Cummings, Alexander, 39

"Andrew **Cunningham** of Boston and Some of His Descendants" (Cunningham), 85

Cunningham, Henry Winchester, 85

Curtis, Henry B., 56

Curtis, Mary, 134

Custom House, Boston: crew list records, 46

Daly, Marie E., 16

"Elizabeth **Danson** and Her Four Husbands, Warren-Sendall-Hayward-Wilson" (Barclay and Barclay), 85

"Judith (**Danson**) Wife of Charles **Crossthwayte**" (Barclay), 85

"Humphrey **Davie**, Merchant of Boston" (Montgomery), 85

Davis, Amasa, 32, 33, 49–50

Davis, Caleb, 51, 53; papers of, 52

Davis, Charlotte Pease, 77

Davis, Walter Goodwin, 79, 85

Dawes, Thomas, Esq., 114

death records, 3, 4, 16, 133; 17th century included in Record Commissioners Reports, 3; sexton's bills, 3; obituaries, 3; estate notices, 3; church records, 3; diaries, 3; vital records, 3; cemeteries, 3; microfilm copies at New England Historic Genealogical Society, Boston Public Library, and Family History Libraries of the Church of Jesus Christ of Latter Day Saints, 4

"Deaths in Boston: Decedents Reported in the *Boston Medical and Surgical Journal,* 1828–1829" (March), 3

Deaths in Boston 1700–1799 (Dunkle and Lainhart), 3

"Old Boston Families: The **Deblois** Family" (Eaton), 85

DeMaraco, William M., 71

Deming, William, 115

Dennis, Maria F., 28

Dennis, Ryan P., 70

Denver, Patrick: undertaker, 16

Dexter, John Haven, 42

Dickenson, Eliphalet, 26

Dickenson, Mary, 26

Digman, James, 139

Dillon, Nellie J., 61

Diocesan Library and Archives, Episcopal Diocese of Massachusetts, The, 13, 92

Directory of American Libraries with Genealogy or Local History Collection (Filby), 91

Directory of Massachusetts Place Names (Davis), 77

dismission records (church), 9

divorce: records, 60, 95–97; heard in county courts, 95; heard in General Court, 95; heard in Court of Assistance, 95

"Divorce and the Changing Status of Women in Eighteenth-Century Massachusetts" (Cott), 95

Documentary History of Chelsea, Including the Boston Precincts of Winnisimmet, Rumney Marsh and Pullen Point, 1624–1824 (Chamberlain), 81

Dodge, George E., 141

Dodge, Kate E., 141

Dodge, Lyda Ann, 141

Dodge, William, 141

"**Dommett** Family in Boston, A" (Holman), 85

Donnilson, Mary, 39

Donovan, Margaret, 134, 135

Dorchester Town Records, 1632–1691, 81

Dorsey, Minnie, 139

Dorvick, Edward, 140

"Colonel Thomas **Doty** of Cape Cod, Plymouth, Boston and Stoughton, Mass." (Barclay), 85

Downeing, Emanuel, 115

Downes, Fred R., 68

Downes, William, 51

Downs, William, 9

"Francis **Dowse** of Boston and His Ten Daughters" (Coddington), 85

Drake, Samuel Gardner, 2, 31, 77

Duffy, Mark, 13

Dun, Joseph, 39

Dunkle, Robert J., 7, 15, 82

Dwight, Michael, 38

Dwight, Rachel, 38

Dwight, Samuel, 38

Eaton, Arthur Wentworth Hamilton, 84, 85, 86

Eaton, Rev. W.H., 13

Ehrenfried, Albert, 14

Eichberg, Julius, 63

Eighth Church (Hollis Street Church), 10

"Daughters of Simon **Eire** of Watertown and Boston, Mass., The" (Anderson), 85

Eleventh Church (School Street, or Rev. Andrew Croswell's Church), 10

Eliot, Andrew, Jr., 114

Ellis, Charles Mayo, 82

Ellis, John, 61, 68

Ellis, Rev. Dr., 142

English, William, 139

Essex Genealogist, The, 21, 113

Ethnics and Enclaves: Boston's Italian North End (DeMarco), 71

Eustis, William, Esq., 114

Family History Libraries of the Church of Jesus Christ of Latter Day Saints (FHL): birth, marriage and death records, 4; holds land records of Suffolk Co., 35; records of Supreme Judicial Court, 37; Records of Court of Admiralty, 38; records of Court of Common Pleas, 39; holds city directories, 31; records from institutions, 131–41

Farber, Daniel: gravestone collection, 16

Farber, Jesse Lye: gravestone collection, 16

Farber Gravestone Collection, 16

Farmer, Paul, 24, 114

"In Search of **Fayerweather**: The Fayerweather Family of Boston" (Carney), 85

Federal Street Church: *see* Arlington Street Church

Felton, Luther, 50

Ferrin, John, 139

"Few Deaths in Boston, A" (Ullmann), 4

Field, Sarah, 39

Fifth Church (New North Church), 10

Filby, P. William, 91

Finding Italian Roots (Colletta), 71

Fines, Henrietta S., 61

Finlayson, Angus, 29

"Four Blessing Sisters, The" [**Firmage**] (Davis), 85

First Baptist Church, 8, 78

First Baptist Church, Roxbury, 9

First Boston City Directory (1789) Including Extensive Annotations by John Haven Dexter (1791–1876), 42

First Christian Church, 8

First Church in Boston, 3, 10, 78; records of in Record Commissioners Report, 7; importance of record keeping by, 7

First Church, Charlestown, 8

First Church, Dorchester, 9

First Church, Second Parish, 8

First Church, West Roxbury, 9

First Universalist Church, 8

Fiske, Jane Fletcher, 84, 89

Fitzpatrick's Boston, 1846–1866: John Bernard Fitzpatrick, Third Bishop of Boston (O'Connor), 2, 79

"Cotton **Flack** of Boston, Mass." (Sprague), 85

"Focus on Boston" (Anderson), 2, 36

"Focus on Boston First Church" (Anderson), 2

Foley, William E., 28

Foote (ffoote), Joshua, 115

Forbes, Allan, 71

Forbes, H., 51

Forbes, Harriette M., 16; gravestone collection of, 16

Ford (fford), Eliza, 22

Ford, Joseph, 73

Ford, Perslla (Priscilla), 73

Ford, Simeon, 134

Forest Hills Cemetery, 15

Formisano, Ronald P., 77

Forty of Boston's Historic Houses. A Brief Illustrated Description of the Residences of Historic Characters of Boston who have Lived in or Near the Business Section, 75

Forty of Boston's Immortals: Showing Illustrations and Giving a Brief Sketch of Forty Men of the Past Whose Work Entitle Them to a Niche in a Boston Hall of Fame, 76

Foster, John W., 68

Fourth Church (Brattle Street, Brattle Square, or Manifesto Church), 8, 10

Foy, Martin, 70

Fracker, Stanley Black, 86

"Descendants of Thomas **Fracker**, Shipbuilder, of Boston, The" (Fracker), 86

Fradd, Brandon, 83

Frank, Joseph, 46

French Huguenot Church, 10

"Some Descendants of John **Furness** of Boston, Mass." (Belknap), 86

Gainer, Thomas, 116

Gallopp, John, 114

Gardner-Wescott, Mr., 77

Garman, Leo H., 90

Garrison, Angeline, 131

Garrison, Henry, 131

Garrison, Mary Makeley, 131

Gazetteer of Massachusetts, A (Hayward), 9

Genealogical Data Extracted from the Boston Selectmen Minutes, 1736–1775 (Burkett), 21

Genealogical Dictionary of Maine and New Hampshire (Noyes, Libby. and Davis), 79

Genealogies and Estates of Charlestown, In the County of Middlesex and Commonwealth of Massachusetts, 1629–1818, The (Wyman), 81

Genealogist's Handbook for New England Research (Melnyk), 79, 91

General Court (Massachusetts Bay Colony), 37

"General Index to Compiled Military Service Records of Revolutionary War Soldiers," 43

George Marshall (ship), 65

"Old Boston Families: The Family of Capt. John **Gerrish**" (Eaton), 86

"Wife of Thomas **Gilbert** of Boston, The" (Hodgman), 86

Gillam (Gillum) (Gellom) (Gilam), Benjamin, 22, 114, 115, 116, 117

Gillam, Edward, 114, 117

Gillam, Robert, 114

Gillespie, Alice, 65

Gillette, Harvey. 29

Godfrey, Ellen, 132

Godfrey, John, 132

Godfrey, Mary, 132, 133

Goss, K. David, 43

Gosse, Phillip, 20

Gould, Sarah E., 63

Grace Church, 8

Graham, Mr., 21

Granary Cemetery, 15

Grand Lodge of Masons in Massachusetts, 74; library, 93

Grant, Mary, 28

Gravestone Inscriptions and Records of the Tomb Burials in the Central Burying Ground, Boston Common, and Inscriptions in The South Burying Ground, 15

Gravestone Inscriptions and Records of the Tomb Burials in the Granary Burying Ground, 15

gravestones: photographs of New England, 16; depositories for, 16

Graveyards of Boston, First Volume, Copp's Hill Epitaphs, The (Whitmore), 15

Gray, Mary, 41

Great Fire of 1700, 20

Great Migration Newsletter, 2, 7, 36

Greek Immigrant Passengers (Voultsos), 71

Greene, David L., 89

"Sarah (Jurdain) (Hill) (Sowther) **Greenleaf**" (Barclay), 896

Griffen, Sgt. William, 29

Guide to Massachusetts Cemeteries, A (Lambert), 15

Guide to the Archives of the Archdiocese of Boston (O'Toole), 10, 12, 13

"Guide to the Court Records of Early Massachusetts, A" (Hindus), 37

Guide to the Manuscript Collections of the New England Historic Genealogical Society, 51, 91

Guide to the Parochial Archives of the Episcopal Church in Boston (Duffy), 13

Hall, Catharine, 26

Hall, Willis, 52

"Old Boston Families: The **Haliburton** Family" (Eaton), 86

Ham, George, 135

Hansen, James L., 89

Harris, Gale Ion, 84, 86

Harris, Ruth-Ann M., 69

"Arthur **Harris** of Duxbury, Bridgewater, and Boston, Massachusetts, with an Account of His Apparent Grandson Thomas Harris of Plainfield, Connecticut" (Harris), 86

"James and Sarah (Eliot?) **Harris** of Boston and New London" (Harris), 86

"**Harrises** in Boston Before 1700" (Jones), 86

"More **Harrises** of Boston" (Harris), 86

Hartman, J. Crawford, 84

Harvard Church, Charlestown, 8

Harvard Divinity School Library, 13, 93

Harvard University, Baker Library: collection of business papers, 51

Haskell, John D., 78

Hastings, Abagail, 39

Hawes Place Church, South Boston, 8

Hawkins: *see* **Porter**

Hayes, Dorothea C., 61

Hayes, Otis H., 61

Hayward, John, 9

"Anthony **Haywood** of Boston" (Loeser), 86

Hazzard, Robert, 139

Hebrew College Library, 93

"**Hedge-Ingoldsbee-Lothrop** Relationships" (Barclay), 86

Hibbins, William, 115

Hill, Sally Dean Hamblen, 89

Hills, Thomas, 85

Hindus, Michael S., 37, 96

Historic New England, 93; photographic collection, 73

Historical Data Relating to Counties, Cities and Towns in Massachusetts, 78

Historical Sketch of the Congregational Churches in Massachusetts from 1620 to 1858, A (Clark), 13

Historical Sketch of the Massachusetts Baptist Missionary Society and Convention, 1802–1902 (Eaton), 13

History and Antiquities of Boston . . . from its Settlement 1n 1630, to the Year 1770, The (Drake), 2

History of East Boston, with Biographical Sketches of its Early Proprietors, A (Sumner), 80

History of Matrimonial Institutions, A (Howard), 95

History of Roxbury Town, The (Ellis), 82

History of South Boston (Toomey and Rankin), 80, 82

History of South Boston: formerly Dorchester Neck; Now Ward XII of the City of Boston (Simonds), 80

History of the Town of Dorchester, Massachusetts, 81

History of the Town of Revere, The (Shurtleff), 81

History of Winthrop, Massachusetts, 1630–1952, The (Clark), 82

"Eliphalet **Hitt** (not Hill) of Boston" (Phillips and Richmond), 86

"Notes on Connecticut Families-Sir Charles **Hobby** and His Connecticut Descendants" (Jacobus), 86

Hodgman, Arthur Winifred, 86

Holbrook, Jay Mack, 78

"Notes on the **Hollingsworth**, Hunter, More, and Woodbury Families of Salem, Mass." (Barclay), 86

Hollis Street Church: *see* Eighth Street Church

Hollis Street Church, Boston; Records of Admissions, Baptisms, Marriages and Deaths, 1732–1887 (Dunkle and Lainhart), 7

Holman, Mary Lovering, 85, 88, 89

Holman, Winifred Lovering, 83, 85, 86, 89

Holmes, Joseph, 20

Holy Trinity (German), South End, 12

Home for Destitute Catholic Children, 109–11; and orphans trains, 109, 110

"**Homer-Stevens** Notes, Boston" (Holman), 86

Hopkins, Thomas, 23

Hormadey, Mrs. Quinn, 87

Horton, James Oliver, 78

Horton, Katharine, 40

Horton, Lois E., 78

Hospital at Rainsford Island, 28; records of, 29

Hospital Cottage for Children: records of, 135

Hospital for Epileptics, Monson: records of, 137

Howard, Apolus, 139

Howard, B., Mr. and Mrs., 26

Howard, George Elliott, 95

Hubnocks, Elizabeth, 24

Hundred Boston Orators Appointed By the Municipal Authorities and Other Public Bodies, From 1770 to 1852; Comprising Historical Gleanings, Illustrating the Principles and Progress of Our Republican Institutions, The (Loring), 79

Hunnewell, James F., 81

Hunt, John G., 87, 89

Hunter, John, 39

Hutchinson, Capt., 116

"Ancestry of Katherine Hamby, Wife of Captain Edward **Hutchinson** of Boston, The" (Wilcox), 87

immigrants, 69–71; Irish, 69, 70; Jewish, 70; Greek, 71; Italian, 71; French, 71; Swedish, 71

indenture agreements, 133

"Indentures of Boston's Poor Apprentices: 1734–1805, The" (Towner), 23

Index of Marriages and Deaths in Massachusetts Centinel, 1784–1790, and Columbian Centinel, 1790–1840, 6

Index of Naturalized Voters, from 1857 to 1878; Registrars of Voters, 59

Index to Naturalized Voters, 1878 to 1888, Board of Election Commissioners, 59

Index to Naturalized Voters, 1896 to 1900, Board of Election Commissioners, 59

Index to Naturalized Voters, May 1, 1892 to May 1, 1896, Registrars of Voters, 59

Index of Obituaries in Boston Newspapers, 1704–1800, 5

Index to Obituary Notices in the Boston Transcript, 1875–1899, 6

Index to Obituary Notices in the Boston Transcript, 1900–1930, 6

Index to the Manuscript Censuses of Boston, (Knight), 128

Ingoldsbee: *see* **Hedge**

Inscriptions and Records of The Old Cemeteries in Boston (Dunkle and Lainhart), 15

Inscriptions from the Monuments in the Granary Burial Ground, Tremont Street (Bridgman), 15

Inventory of the Records of the Particular (Congregational) Churches of Massachusetts, The (Worthley), 10

Ipswich Insane Asylum: records of, 131

Israelites in Boston: A Tale Describing the Development of Judaism in Boston (Schlinder), 14

Jackson, Edmund, 115

Jackson, George West, 90

Jackson, Joseph, 114

Jacobs, Donald M., 69

Jacobus, Donald Lines, 86, 87, 88, 89, 90

Jaknbasz, Mary Dominik, 140

Jaknbasz, Sophia: *see* Morrissey, Sophia Jaknbasz

Jaknbasz, Thomas, 140

James, Donald W. Jr., 86

"William **James** of Scituate and Boston, Massachusetts, Shipwright and Quaker" (Myers and James), 87

Jameson, Susan B., 62

Jenkins, John, 41

"Additions and Corrections to **Jepson** Genealogy" (Coddington), 87

"The Parentage of John **Jepson** of Boston, Massachusetts" (Thompson), 87

Jewish Cemetery Association of Massachusetts, 17

Jews of Boston, The (Smith and Sarna), 14, 70

John Haven Dexter's Memoranda of the Town of Boston in the 18th & 19th Centuries (Dunkle and Lainhart), 42

Johnson, Arthur W., 68

Johnson, Francena, 133

Johnson, John H., 133

Johnson, Oren, 133

Johnson, Seth, 139

"Mary Foxe, Wife of Lawrence Hazard and Samuel **Johnson** of Stepney, Middlesex, England, and Boston, Massachusetts" (Mahler and Sanborn), 87

Jones, Edson Salisbury, 88

"Ancestry of John **Jones**, 18th Century Boston, Merchant, The" (Couet), 87

Jones, Roderick Bissell, 86

Jordan, Alice M. (Mrs. Porter), 63

Joslyn, Roger D., 6, 81

Journey Through Boston Irish History, A (Ryan), 70

Kahn, Bonheim, 59

Keenan, Timothy, 135

"Stebbins-**Keene**-Eldredge, Boston, Massachusetts" (Hunt), 87

Keine, Mr., 114

Kelley, Elizabeth, 26

Kelley, James, 26

Kelley, Mary Jane, 26

Kelly, Patrick, 70

Kendall, John, 140

Kendall, Mary Agnes, 140

Kendall, Mary Smith, 140

Kenney, Rosanne, 26

Kien, August, 62, 68

Kien, Theresa M.J., 62, 68

Kien, William, 68

"**Kilby** Notes" (Holman), 87

Kimball, Alice, 140

Kimball, Helen, 140

King, Helen Josephine, 26

King, Jane Elizabeth, 26

King, William, 116

King's Chapel, 8, 10; cemetery, 15

Kingsbury, Clara, 26

Kirker, Harold, 2, 78

Knapp, Josiah, 56

Knights, Peter R., 78, 128

Koppler, John Valentine, 40

Krieger, Alex, 78

Lainhart, Ann S., 7, 15, 42, 82, 83, 84, 85, 90

"Deputy-Governor Stephen Goodyear of New Haven, Reverent John Bishop of Stanford, and the **Lake** and **Watts** Families of Boston" (Jacobus), 87

"English Ancestry of the **Lake** Family of Boston, Massachusetts, and of Sir Edward

Lake, Baronet, of England, The" (Peck), 87

Lally, James, 68

Lally, Martin, 68

Lambert, David Allen, 15

land records: Suffolk County, 35–36

Lane, William, 22

"Descendants of Philip and John **Langdon** of Boston, The" (Alger), 87

"Philip and John **Langdon** of Boston" (Hormandy), 87

Larger Hope: The First Century of the Universalist Church in America, 1770–1870, The (Miller), 14

Law in Colonial Massachusetts, 1630–1800, 37

Leahey, Daniel, 60

Learned, Clarence E., 67

Leaverns, George G., 135

Leavitt, Luella K., 61

Lee, John, 22

Lee, Thomas Amory, 87

"Old Boston Families: The **Lee** Family" (Lee), 87

"**Legare** Notes" (Holman), 87

Lesure, Frank G., 83

"Second Wife of Hudson **Leverett**, The" (Wead), 87

Leverit, John, 115

Levesque, George A., 79

Libby, Charles Thornton, 79

List of Maps of Boston, Published Between 1614 and 1822, Reprint of Appendix J. Annual Report of the City Engineer, 79

"List of seamen and officers from Boston in the U.S. Navy (1861–1865)," 44

Littlewood, Thomas, 114

Loeser, Rudolf, 86

Log of the State Street Trust Company: Containing a Description of its Colonial Banking Rooms, its Ship Models, Quaint Furnishings, Rare Prints of Ships and Views of Boston and Other New England Towns-Including a Story of the 'Lamp Shade Fleet' and Sketches of the Company's Staff, with a Story of the National Union Bank and a Chapter on the Significance of State Street as a Business Centre, 76

Loring, James Spear, 79

Lothrop, Harriet E., 61

Lothrop: *see* **Hedge**

Love, Robert, 39

Lowe, Mrs. Nathaniel, 135

Lyman, E.N., 137

Lyman School for Boys: records of, 135, 139

Lyn, John, 39

Lyn, Royal, 39

Lynch, Frank M., 60

Lynde Street Church, 10

Lyon, Anna, 38

MacKay, Robert E., 43

Magennis, Margaret J., 61

"'Magistracy fit and necessary': A Guide to the Massachusetts Court System, A" (Menard), 37

Mahler, Leslie, 87, 88, 89

Makeley, Jacob, 131

Makeley, Mary: *see* Garrison, Mary

"Ancestry of the Royally Descended **Mansfields** of the Massachusetts Bay, The" (Anderson, Brandon, and Reed), 87

Manuscript Collections of the Congregational Library at Boston: A Survey (Morgan), 13

Mapping Boston (Krieger and Cobb), 78

March, David F., 3

Marey, Joseph, 140

marriage records, 4; 17th and 18th century included in Record Commissioners Reports, 3; microfilm copies at New England Historic Genealogical Society, Boston Public Library and Family History Libraries of the Church of Jesus Christ of Latter Day Saints, 4

Marsh, Frederick E., 137

Marsh, Mrs. Frederick E., 137

Marsh, William C., 137

Martin, Catherine, 133

Martin, George W., 67

Mason, Jonathan, Esq., 114

Mason, Rev. Charles, 30

Massachusetts Archives: *see* Massachusetts State Archives

Massachusetts Bay Colony: courts of, 37; divorce records, 95

Massachusetts Episcopalians, 1607–1957 (Tyng), 13

Massachusetts Genealogical Research (Schweitzer), 80

Massachusetts Historical Society (MHS), 1; records of Overseers of the Poor, 24; collection of business papers, 51; Caleb Davis papers, 52; library, 93

Massachusetts in the Army and Navy during the War of 1861–65, 44

Massachusetts Officers and Soldiers in the French and Indian Wars, 1755–1756 (Goss and Zarowin), 43

Massachusetts Officers and Soldiers, 1723–1743, Dummer's War to the War of Jenkins' Ear (Stachiw), 43

Massachusetts Officers in the French and Indian Wars, 1748–1763 (Voye), 43

Massachusetts Reformatory for Women, Framingham: records of, 140

Massachusetts School for Idiotic and Feeble-Minded Youth: records of, 28, 29, 136

Massachusetts Society of Mayflower Descendants, 93

Massachusetts Soldiers and Sailors of the Revolutionary War, 43

Massachusetts Soldiers in the French and Indian Wars, 1744–1755 (MacKay), 43

Massachusetts Sources, Part I: Boston, New Bedford, Springfield, Worcester, 77

Massachusetts Special Collections (Trinkaus-Randall), 80, 91

Massachusetts State Archives, 1, 93; contain records of Superior Court of Judicature, 4; records of institutions for the ill and poor, 24, 131–41; records of the Supreme Judicial Court, 37; records of the Court of Admiralty, 38; records of the Court of Common Pleas, 39; military records, 43; and census records, 55, 57; divorce records, 94, 95

Massachusetts State Board of Insanity: records of, 136

Massachusetts State Hospital records: Boston, 135; Danvers, 136; Grafton, 136; Foxborough, 137; Medfield, 137; Northampton, 137; Taunton, 137; Westborough, 138

Massachusetts State Nautical School: records of, 139

Massachusetts Supreme Judicial Court, 37

Massachusetts Tax Valuation List of 1771, 49

Massachusetts: A Bibliography of Its History (Haskell), 78

Matson, Thomas, 114

"Elizabeth Thomas, Wife of Joshua **Matson** and Sampson **Moor** of Boston" (Wakefield), 87

Matthews, Russell V., 62

Matthews, Virginia W., 62

Matthews, W., 51

May, John, 39

Mayflower Descendant, The (Williams, 39

Mayors of Boston—An Illustrated Epitome of Who the Mayors Have Been and What They Have Done, 75

McBean, Edward O., 61

McCarty, Patrick, 132

McCauley, Cornelius, 138

McCormick, Andrew, 68

McCracken, George E., 84, 88

McDaniel, Dr., 135

McFarlane, Grace, 26–27

McGillicuddy, John, 136

McGillicuddy, Mary, 136

McGlaughlin, W.G., 13

McHugh, James, 60

McIntire, Sarah, 26

McKenzy, Jonathan, 20

McTeer, Francis Davis, 88

Means, John, 39

Melnyk, Marcia D., 79, 91

Memorial History of Boston, Including Suffolk County, Massachusetts, 1630–1880, The (Winsor), 2, 80

Memorials of The Dead in Boston: Containing Exact Transcripts of Inscriptions on the Sepulchral Monuments in the King's Chapel Burial Ground, in the City of Boston (Bridgman), 15

Menand, Catherine S., 37

Merrill, John, 24

Metcalf, Arthur, 62

Metcalf, Bernice E., 62

Military Records of Hospital Care, Rainsford Island, Boston, 1854–1866: records of, 136

military records, 43–47; *see also* various depositories

militias, 43

Miller, Russell E., 14

ministers: list of Boston up to 1846, 99–107

Mitchell, Caroline, 139

Mitchell, Frederic A., 139

Mitchell, John A., 139

Montcrieff, Sarah, 39

Montgomery, Robert H., 84, 85, 88, 90

Moor, Abigail, 39

Moor, Daniel, 39

Moor, Joseph, 39

Moor, Joshua, 39

Moor, Lucretia, 39

Moor: *see* **Matson**

Morgan, Mary Frederica Rhinelander, 13

Moriarty, G. Andrews, 86

Morrissey, Sophia Jaknbasz, 140

"John **Morse** of Boston" (Montgomery), 88

Morse, Samuel, 139

Most Holy Redeemer (St. Nicholas), East Boston, 12

Mt. Auburn Cemetery, 15, 16

Mulhearn, Bridget, 28

Mulhearn, Michael, 28

Mulhearn, Sarah, 28

Mullaby, William, 59–60

Mullin, George, 137

Mulvey, John, 46

Munjey, Josiah, 20

Murphy, Dominick, 42

Murphy, Edward J., 42

Murphy, John, 42

Murphy, John J., 42

Murphy, John P., 42

Murphy, John T., 42

Murphy, John England, 70

Murphy, Margaret H., 70

Murphy, Patrick J., 42

Murphy, Thomas, 42

Murphy, Thomas J., 42

Murphy, Timothy B., 70

Murphy, Timothy J., 42

Musculus, Elizabeth, 62

Musculus, William F., 62

Myers, Marya C., 87, 89

National Archives and Records Administration, 46; holds military service records and draft cards, 44; military pension indexes, 44; holds Seamen's Protection Papers or Applications for Seamen's Certificate of American Citizenship, 46; holds crew lists from Boston Customs House, 46; passenger lists for Port of Boston, 65; holds naturalization records, 67

National Archives, Northeast Region, 93

National Union Catalog of Manuscript Collections, The, 51

naturalization, 77; records, 67–68; female immigrants, 68

naval militia, 47

naval records, 43–47

Needham, Jonathan, 20

New Brick Church, 8, 10

New England Diaries, 1602–1800, A Descriptive Catalog of Diaries, Orderly Books, and Sea Journals (Forbes), 51

New England Dissent, 1630–1833, The Baptists and Separation of Church and State (McGlaughlin), 13

"New England Gravestones, 1653–1800" (Forbes), 16

New England Historic Genealogical Society (NEHGS), 1, 42; birth, marriage and death records at, 4; records of churches, 8; holds "New England Gravestones" collection, 16; records of Overseers of the Poor, 24; holds admission to Boston City Hospital, 30, holds land records of Suffolk Co., 35; holds city directories, 41, 42; and military records, 43; tax records, 49, 50; and census records, 55; and passenger lists for Port of Boston, 65

New England Historic Genealogical Society Library, 94

New England Historical and Genealogical Register, The (NEGHR), 3, 9, 31, 42, 55

New England Quaker Meetings: records of, 13

New Jerusalem Church, 8

New North Church, 8, 9, 10

New North Church, Boston, 1714–1799, The (Wyman), 7

New South Church, 8

Newcomb, Isaac G., 67

Newsletter of the Massachusetts Genealogical Council, 6

Nielsen, Donald M., 88

Ninth Church (West or Lynde Street Church), 10

Nixson, Kris, 46

Noble, John, 38

Nolan, John L., 46

Nolan, Patric, 26

Norden, August, 46

Norton, Dr. Eben, 136

Noyes, Charles P., 84

Noyes, Sybil, 79

Nyston, John, 46

obituaries, 5

O'Brien, Elizabeth, 133

O'Brien, Maria, 133

O'Brien, Martin, 133

O'Brien, William, 132

O'Connor, Thomas H., 2, 79

O'Connor, Thomas H., 79

Odell, Willis P., 141

Odline, John, 115

O'Donnell, Catherine, 134

O'Dwyer, Elizabeth C., 62

O'Dwyer, Myles, 62

"Probable Ancestry of Margaret **Ogilvie** of Boston" (McTeer and Warner), 88

O'Keefe, B. Emer, 69

Old North Church, 8, 10, 78

Old Shipping Days in Boston, 76

Old South Church, 8, 78

Oliver, Andrew, 7

"English Origins of Thomas **Oliver** of Boston, The" (Mahler), 88

Oman, Matthew, 60

orphans' trains, 109, 110

Other Merchants and Sea Captains of Old Boston: Being More Information About the Merchants and Sea Captains of Old Boston Who Played Such an Important Part in Building up the Commerce of New England Together with Some Quaint and Curious Stories of the Sea, 76

Other Statues of Boston: Reproductions of Other Statues of Boston as a Sequel to Our Brochure of 1946, 75

Otis, Harrison G., 114

O'Toole, James M., 10, 12, 13

"Descendants of the Duke of Montrose, the Prince of Monaco, and Princess Schwarzenberg, from Rev. John **Oxenbridge** of Boston, Mass." (Coddington), 88

Page, Mary, 26

"**Papillons** of Boston and Bristol, The" (Wait), 88

Park, Laurence, 89

Park Street Church, 8

Parke, John, 115

Parker, William, 29

"Family of George **Parkhurst** of Watertown and Boston, Mass., The" (Jones), 88

Parkinson, Lizzie, 24
Parkinson, Samuel, 24
Particular, Nothing (hospital patient), 131
Partridge, George, 37
Partridge, Capt. Samuel, 24
passenger lists, 65–66, 77
paupers: burials, 16; records of, 22–30
Pavonia (ship), 65
Peabody, James Bishop, 7
Peck, Allyn S., 87
pension records: military, 43
"People of Color in Massachusetts States Census, 1855–1865," 57
Perkins Institution and Massachusetts Asylum for the Blind, Watertown: records of, 138
Permits for Demolished Buildings: records of, 73
Perry, An, 22
Phillips Church, South Boston, 8
Phillips, Ralph David, 86
"**Phippen** Family and the Wife of Nathan Gold of Fairfield, Connecticut, The" (Jacobus), 88
photographic collections: held by Bostonian Society, Boston Public Library, Historic New England, 73
Pierce, Richard Andrew, 16
Pierce, Richard D., 7
"Ruth **Pierce's** Five Husbands" (Wead), 88
Pierpont, Joshua, 52
Pierpont, Robert, 51, 52
Pilgrims of Boston and Their Descendants, The (Bridgman), 15
Pilots and Pilot Boats of Boston Harbor: Presenting Stories and Illustrations of the Skilled, Resourceful Men of Stout Hearts Who, with Their Trim, Weatherly Boats of Sturdy Construction, have Played such an Important Role in the Maritime Life of Boston, 76
Pine Street Church, 8
Pitman, H. Minot, 84, 89
Pitts Street Chapel, 8
Plain People of Boston, 1830–1860: A Study in City Growth, The (Knights), 78
Plymouth Colony: divorce records, 95
Pope, Otis, 56
"Port Arrivals and Immigrants to the City of Boston, 1715–1716 and 1762–1769,"

in Boston Records Commissioners Reports, 21
"The **Porter** and **Hawkins** Families of Boston" (Moriarty), 86
"Michael **Powell** of Dedham and Boston" (Anderson), 88
Pray, Adelaide, 61
Pray, James H., 61
Price, Michael, 2, 69, 80
probate courts: jurisdiction over divorce, 96
probate records, 31–33; handled by Suffolk County, 31; inventories included in , 32
Province and Court Records of Maine, 37
Publication of The Colonial Society of Massachusetts, 23, 79
Purchase Street Church, 8
Puritan Boston and Quaker Philadelphia, Two Protestant Ethics and the Spirit of Class, Authority and Leadership (Baltzell), 77
Pychon, George, 23

Quakers in Boston (Selleck), 14
Quin, John, 70
"English Origins of Edmund **Quincy** of Boston and His Servants, Thomas and Katherine (Greene) Meakins, The" (Mahler), 88

Ranger, Samuel, 40
Rankin, Edward P.B., 80
Rasmussen, James Anthony, 84, 88
"Rainsford Island Hospital Register (1854–1865)," 44
"Edward **Raynsford** of Boston: English Ancestry and American Descendants" (Rasmussen), 88
"New Light on Esdras **Reade**, Tailor" (McCracken), 88
Record Commissioner Reports, 3, 19–22; includes 17th century birth, marriage, and death records, 3; includes baptismal records of First Church, 3; includes 18th century birth and marriage records, 3; records of selectmen and town meetings, 19, 20; Aspinwall Notorial Records, 21; Book of Possessions (land), 36; and census records, 55
Records of Boston Selectmen: in Boston Records Commissioners Reports, 20
"Records of the Churches of Boston, The" (Dunkle and Lainhart), CD of, 7, 8
Records of the Court Assistants of the Colony of Massachusetts Bay, 37

Records of the First Church at Dorchester in New England, 1636–1734, 81

Records of the First Church in Charlestown, Massachusetts, 1632–1789 (Hunnewell), 81

Records of the First Church of Boston (Pierce), 7

Records of the Governor and Company of Massachusetts Bay in New England 1628–1686 (Shurtleff), 37

Records of the Massachusetts Superior Court And Its Predecessors: An Inventory and Guide, The (Hindus), 96

Records of the Massachusetts Volunteer Militia Called Out by the Governor of Massachusetts to Suppress a Threatened Invasion During the War of 1812–1814, 43–44

Records of Trinity Church, Boston, 1728–1830 (Oliver and Peabody), 7

Redding, Lucy M.A., 63

Reed, Paul C., 87

Reed, Sampson, 114

Registrar of Vital Records and Statistics, 94

Registry of Births, Marriages, and Deaths (Boston City Hall), 5

Registry of Deeds: Suffolk County Courthouse, 35; indexes, 35

Registry of Vital Records and Statistics (for state of Massachusetts), 5; divorce records, 96

Renott, Arria Sargent, 26

Renott, Jane Flagg, 26

Report on the Custody and Condition of the Public Records of Parishes, Towns, and Counties (Wright): and church records, 9, 21

repositories (for Boston area), 91–94

Resources for Jewish Genealogy in the Boston Area (Blatt), 17, 70, 77

"**Revere** Family, The" (Nielsen), 88

"Reverend James Allen's Church Census of 1688" (Sanborn), 7

Revolutionary War, 43

Rhodes, James Thomas, 60, 68

Rhodes, Walter J., 60, 68

Richards, Marietta F., 141

Richmond, Francis Sears, 86

Riley, John, 140

Risby, Robert, 116

Robie, Dr. W.F., 136

Robinson, Mary (Robertson?) 29

Rochford, George J., 132

Rochford, John C., 132

Rochford, Mary, 132

Rochford, Mary E., 132

"James **Rogers** of Boston (1729–1793), His Daughter Elizabeth (Rogers) Roby and their Jepson Link" (Schoeffler), 88

Rohrbach, Lewis Bunker, 49

Rossi, Anthony J., 60

Rowan, William M., 60

Rowson, Susan, 26

Roxbury Land Records and Church Records, 82

Ruddock, John, 114

Russell, Thomas, 40

Russell, William, 40

Rutman, Darrett B., 2, 80

St. Augustine Cemetery, 16

St. Joseph Cemetery, Roxbury, 16

St. Joseph, Roxbury, 12

St. Mary, Charlestown, 12

St. Mary, North End, 12

St. Matthew's Church, South Boston, 8

St. Patrick, South End, 12

St. Paul's Church, 8

St. Peter and Paul, South Boston, 12

St. Stephen (St. John the Baptist), North End, 12

Salter, Anna, 39

"Notes on Some Immigrants from Otery St. Mary Devon—**Salter**" (Holman), 88

Sammarco, Anthony Mitchell, 2, 69, 80

Samuel Crocker Lawrence Library and Museum: and Masonic holdings, 74

Sanborn, Melinde Lutz, 7, 55, 87

Sand Banks Catholic Cemetery, 16

Sanderson: see **Vyall**

"Some Descendants of Digory **Sargent** of Boston and Worcester, Mass." (Woods), 88

Sargent, Selina, 27

Sarna, Jonathan, 14, 70

"Old Boston Families: The **Savage** Family" (Park), 89

"**Sawdy** Family of Boston, Rhode Island, and Points West, The" (Fiske), 89

Sayer, Jacob, 22

"**Scate-Skeath** Family of Boston; Rebecca, Wife of Ebenezer Allen of Bridgewater, The" (Barclay), 89

Schlesinger, Keith R., 128

Schlinder, Solomon, 14

Schoeffler, William H., 88

Scholtz, Caroline, 27

School Board elections: women permitted to vote in, 61

School Street Church: *see* Eleventh Church

Schweitzer, George K., 80

Scott, Minnie O., 61

Seamen's Protection Papers, 46

Search for Missing Friends, Irish Immigrant Advertisements Placed in the Boston Pilot, 69

Second National Bank of Boston, The, 77

Second Baptist Church, 8

Second Church: *see* Old North Church

Second Congregational Church, Charlestown, 8

Second Universalist Church, 8

Selleck, George A., 14

1798 Direct Tax: in Record Commissioners Series, 49

Seventh Church (New Brick Church), 10

"English Ancestry of Philip Watson Challis of Ipswich, Massachusetts, with an Account of His Uncle Thomas **Sharpe**, Briefly Resident at Boston, Massachusetts, The" (Mahler), 89

Shattuck, Frederick Cheever, 53

Sheldon, Harry, 132

Sheldon, Horatio, 132

Sheldon, Maria, 132

Shurtleff, Benjamin, 81

Shurtleff, Nathaniel B., 37

Silva, Frank, 134

Simonds, Thomas C., 80

Simons, D. Brenton, 51, 85

"Family of Pilgrim **Simpkins** of Boston, The" (Holman), 89

Sinko, Peggy Tuck, 128

Sixth Church (New South Church), 10

"Ancestry of Joan Legard, Grandmother of the Rev. William **Skepper/Skipper** of Boston, Massachusetts" (Hansen), 89

"**Skepper** Family, The" (Holman), 89

Slowe, Catherine, 61, 68

Slowe, Michael, 61, 68

Smallage, Martha, 23

Smith, Ellen, 14, 70

Smith, George Franklin, 140

Smith, Lucinda, 134

Smith, Mary: *see* Kendall, Mary Smith

Smith, Maud L., 139

Smith, Mrs. M.L., 27

Smith, Mr. and Mrs. N., 26

"Some **Snellings** of Boston" (Pitman), 89

Society for Prevention of Cruelty to Children, 110

Society for the Preservation of New England Antiquities (SPNEA): *see* Historic New England

Society of Colonial Wars in the Commonwealth of Massachusetts, 43

Soldiers in King Phillip's War (Bodge), 43

Some Events of Boston and Its Neighbors, 75

Some Interesting Boston Events, 75

Some Merchants and Sea Captains of Old Boston: Being a Collection of Sketches of Notable Men and Mercantile Houses Prominent During the Early Half of the Nineteenth Century in the Commerce and Shipping of Boston, 76

Some Ships of the Clipper Ship Era: Their Builders, Owners and Captains. A Glance at an Interesting Phase of the American Merchant Marine so far as it Relates to Boston, 76

Some Statues of Boston: Some Reproductions of Some of the Statues for which Boston is Famous, with Information Concerning the Personalities and Events so Memorialized, 75

South Boston: My Home Town, The History of an Ethnic Neighborhood (O'Connor), 79

"Bancroft Addenda with **Sowther** and Gilbert Notes" (Hunt), 89

Spanish-American War/Philippine Insurrection, 46

Spearwater, T.W., 46

Sprague, Waldo Chamberlain, 85

Stachiw, Myron O., 43

Stamp, Mr., 21

Staples, W.L., 46

State Almshouse, Monson: records of, 131

State Almshouse, Tewksbury, 131: records of, 28, 134

State Board of Lunacy and Charity, 133

State Industrial School for Girls: records of, 135

State Library of Massachusetts, 94

State Primary School at Monson, 133; admission forms, 133; hospital records, 134

State Reform School, Westborough *see* Lyman School for Boys

State Sanatorium, Rutland: records of, 137

State Street Bank and Trust Company: historic publications, 75–77

State Street Events: A Brief Account of Diverse Notable Persons and Sundry Stirring Events Having to do with the History of this Ancient Street, 76

State Street: A Brief Account of a Boston Way, 76

Statistics of the United States Direct Tax of 1798, as Assessed on Boston; and The Names of the Inhabitants of Boston in 1790, as Collected for the First National Census: in Boston Records Commissioners Reports, 20

Steele, Frank, 134

Stevens, William, Jr., 134

Stevens: *see* **Homer**

Stones Speak: Irish Place Names from Inscriptions in Boston's Mount Calvary Cemetery, The (Pierce), 16

Story of the Irish in Boston, The (Cullen), 70

Stratton, R., 20

Suffolk County Probate and Family Court, 94

Suffolk County Registry of Deeds, 94

Suffolk County Sheriff's Records, 1799–1916, 139

Suffolk County Wills, Abstracts of the Earliest Wills Upon Record in the County of Suffolk, Massachusetts, from The New England Historical and Genealogical Register, 31

Suffolk County: probate records, 31–33; "New Series," 32

Sullivan, Daniel, 60, 134

Sullivan, Honora, 134

Sullivan, Jeremiah, 134

Sullivan, John, 134

Sullivan, Julia, 132

Sullivan, Margaret, 134

Sullivan, Michael, 134

Sullivan, Timothy, 134

Sullivan, William, 132

Sumner, William H., 80

Sunderson: *see* **Vyall**

Superior Court of Judicature, 37; records at Massachusetts Archives, 4; "Court Files Suffolk Births, Marriages, and Deaths Jan 1637/8 to Aug 1774," 4

Superior Courts of Massachusetts: jurisdiction over divorce, 96

Supreme Judicial Court of Massachusetts: divorce records, 95; jurisdiction over divorce, 96

Swansbury, Richard, 22, 114

Swedish City Directory of Boston, 1881, A (Wretlind), 71

Swift, Mrs. William, 29

Swith, Rev. S., 26

"Stephen and Hannah (Place) **Talby** of Boston, Massachusetts, with Notes on Hannah Sunderland Wife of Matthew Armstrong and Abraham Gording of Boston" (Hill), 89

Tarlton, William B.: census enumerator, 125, 126

tax lists, 49–50

Tax Payers, Town of Dorchester, 1849–1869, 81

Tax Valuation Records: at Boston City Archives, 50

Taylor, Richard H., 13

Teachers' records, 63–64

Temporary Home for the Destitute, 24

Tenth Church (Samuel Mather's Church), 10

Terry, Ann, 26

Terry, Seth, 26

Tewksbury Asylum for Chronic Insane: records of, 138

Third Church (Old South Church), 10

Third Parish of Roxbury, 8

Thomas, Isaiah, 44

Thompson, Andrew J., 62

Thompson, Katherine, 62

Thompson, Neil D., 87

Thompson, William, 28

Thwing, Annie Haven, 32, 36, 80

"Thwing Collection," 36; abstracts of Boston town, land and probate records, 32

"Notes—**Thwing**" (Holman), 88

Tierney, Edward, 70

Tierney, Thomas, 70

Tisdale, Ruth M., 62

Todd, Neil: and list of ministers, 9

Toomey, John J., 80, 82

Town of Roxbury, Its Memorable Persons and Places, The, 82

Town Records of Roxbury, Massachusetts, 1647–1730 (Dunkle and Lainhart), 82

Towner, Lawrence, 23

Townsends, Capt. 117

Trask, William B., 31

Tremont Temple Baptist Church, 142

Trinkaus-Randall, Gregor, 80, 91

Tudor, William, 114

"Tracking Benjamin **Tuell(s)** through Eighteenth-Century Massachusetts and Rhode Island" (Myers), 89

Turner, John, 115

"Children of Richard **Tuttle** of Boston, The" (Greene), 89

Twelfth Congregational Church, 8

Tyng, D., 14

Ullmann, Helen Schatvet, 4

University of Massachusetts at Boston, Joseph P. Healey Library, 94

Upham, William, 140

"'Urban Finding Aid' for the Federal Census, An" (Schlesinger), 128

"Urban Finding Aid for Manuscript Census Searchers" (Schlesinger and Sinko), 128

Usher, Langdon, 113

Utinocks, Eliza, 24

Varney, George W., 89

"Thomas **Varney** of Boston and Some of His Descendants" (Varney), 88

"Wife of Samuel **Vial**, The" (Wead), 89

Vital Records of Charlestown, Massachusetts, to the Year 1850 (Joslyn), 81

Vital Records of the Town of Dorchester from 1826–1849, 81

Volume Relating to the Early History of Boston Containing the Aspinwall Notorial Records from 1644 t0 1651, The: in Boston Records Commissioners Reports, 21

Volumes of Partitions and Executions from, 1694 to 1856: Supreme Judicial Court records, 37

Vose, Isaac, 56

voter lists, 59–62

Voultsos, Mary, 71

Voye, Nancy S., 43

"**Vyall-Sanderson-Sunderland**, Boston, Mass." (Wead), 88

Wait, Estelle Wellwood, 88

Wakefield, Robert S., 87

Walker, Robert, 23

"Double Davenports: Descendants of James and Mary (**Walker**) Davenport of Boston" (Willcox and Willcox), 89

"Robert **Walker** of Boston, Massachusetts" (Coddington), 90

"Jilting of Samuel **Walker**, Mariner of Boston, The" (Hill), 89

Wallace, Ella, 62

Wallace, John L., 62

War of 1812, 43–44

Ward, Benjamin, 115

Ware, Delia B., 137

Warner, Frederick C., 87

Warning Out in New England, 1656–1817 (Benton), 38

Warren, John, Esq., 114

Warren: *see* **Barlow**

"Abigail **Waters**, Wife of Benjamin Walcott" (Barclay and Barclay), 90

Watkins, Walter K., 31

Watson, Edith S., 62

Watson, Joseph, 62

Watts: *see* **Lake**

Wead, Frederick W., 83, 87, 88, 89

"Three Wives of David **Webb** of Boston, Mass., and Wethersfield, Conn., The" (Barnes), 89

"Too Many David **Webbs**" (Lainhart), 89

"Some Descendants of James **Webster**, Brewer, of Boston, MA" (Garman), 90

Weis, Frederick Lewis, 9

"Records of the **West** Family of Boston and Taunton, Mass., and Allied Families" (Jackson), 90

West Church, 8, 10

Wharton, William, 22

Whitmarsh, Nehemiah, 41

Whitmore, William H., 15

"English Ancestry of Samuel **Wilbore** of Boston and William Wilbore of Portsmouth, R.I." (Wilbour), 90

Wilbour, Benjamin Franklin, 90

Wilcox, Wayne Howard Miller, 87

Willcox, Doris Schreiber, 89

Willcox, David Land, 89

William and Mary Quarterly, The, 95

Williams, Alicia Crane, 39, 83

Williams, Elijah, 23

"Nathaniel **Williams** of Boston" (Montgomery), 90

Willis, Jonathan: diary of, 51

"Ancestry and Descendants of Rev. John **Wilson** of Boston, Mass." (Bartlett), 90

"Seaborn **Wilson** and Shoreborn Wilson of Ipswich and Boston, Massachusetts" (Jacobus), 90

Wings, John, 22

Winsor, Justin, 2, 80

Winthrop, Adam, 115

Winthrop, Stephen, 115

Winthrop's Boston, Portrait of A Puritan Town, 1630–1649 (Rutman), 2, 80

women: permitted to vote in school board elections, 61

Wood, Mary, 20

Woods, Henry Ernest, 88

"From One Boston to Another: Notes on the Ancestry of Mary (Jackson) **Woodward**" (Brayton), 90

"Nathaniel **Woodward** of Boston, and Some of His Descendants" (Woodward), 90

Woodward, Sarah C., 63

Woodward, Theron Royal, 90

"Virginia Family of Boston: The **Woodwards**" (Allen), 90

Woodworth-Barnes, Esther Littleford, 84

Worcester Insane Hospital or Lunatic Hospital: records of, 138

Works Progress Administration: and compilation of vital statistics, 6; index of naturalizations, 67

World War I: records, 44, 46

World War II: records, 44, 46

Worthley, Harold Field, 10

Wretlind, Eric, 71

Wright, Carroll D., 9, 21

Wyman, Thomas Bellows, 7, 81

Yankee Destinies, The Lives of Ordinary Nineteenth-Century Bostonians, (Knights), 78

Yankee Ship Sailing Cards: Presenting Reproductions of Some of the Colorful Cards Announcing Ship Sailings in the Days When Boston Ships and Boston Men Were Known in Every Port of the Seven Seas, 76

Young, John, 68

Zarowin, David, 43